EVERGREEN PILOT BOOKS

Chief Editor
A. Norman Jeffares

Advisory Editors
David Daiches   C. P. Snow

W. B. YEATS

Izabel Howard —

Shreveport, La —

W. B. YEATS

Peter Ure

GROVE PRESS, INC.
NEW YORK

First published by Oliver and Boyd Ltd
Edinburgh, Scotland, 1963

Library of Congress Catalog Card Number: 64-10096

First Evergreen Edition 1964

Manufactured in Great Britain

CONTENTS

ACKNOWLEDGMENTS

For permission to quote from W. B. Yeats's verse and prose works, acknowledgments are due to Mr W. B. Yeats, to Macmillan & Co. Ltd, to the Macmillan Company, New York, and to A. P. Watt & Son.

The photograph on the front cover is produced by permission of Radio Times Hulton Picture Library.

ABBREVIATIONS BY WHICH W. B. YEATS'S WORKS ARE REFERRED TO IN THE REFERENCES AT THE END OF EACH CHAPTER

A.	=	*Autobiographies*, London, 1955
C.P.	=	*Collected Poems*, London, 1950
C. Plays	=	*Collected Plays*, London, 1952
C.W.	=	*Collected Works*, Stratford-on-Avon, 1908
E.	=	*Explorations*, London, 1962
E. & I.	=	*Essays and Introductions*, London, 1961
F.P.D.	=	*Four Plays for Dancers*, London, 1921
L.	=	*Letters*, ed. Allan Wade, London, 1954
L.P.	=	*Letters on Poetry to Dorothy Wellesley*, London, 1940
M.	=	*Mythologies*, London, 1958
V. (1925)	=	*A Vision*, London, 1925
V. (1937)	=	*A Vision*, London, 1937

CHAPTER I

BIOGRAPHICAL INTRODUCTION

Yeats gave an account of his earliest years in *Reveries over Childhood and Youth* (1914) and of his young manhood, from 1887 to about 1896, in *The Trembling of the Veil* (1922). These two books are easily his best prose works. They belong, after all, to the period of his great poems, which had begun between 1904 and 1910. They were written at a time when his life and thought, which had so long been subjected to *multiplicity*, "mirror on mirror imaged," as he put it in a late poem, were growing clear and strong in his own imagination. In them the impulse to "arrange all in one clear view," to unbind

> What none can understand,
> What none can have and thrive,
> Youth's dreamy load . . .

expressed itself in the making of patterns and parables out of his experience. He was—or had become—a great connoisseur of personalities, and the autobiographies are not meanly self-centred books; but they are the work of the kind of man whom Yeats called "subjective": one by whom the outer world is recast, as was Othello's, in some creative, inner alembic and so transformed into an arte-fact. Often, after he has given his account of some vivid personality, Wilde, or Lionel Johnson, or John O'Leary, his writing lifts itself on to a level of dramatisation or rhetorical question, which fixes the subject as a represen-tation of Yeats's now defined and saving convictions about man and history. It is the method used in the great personal poems such as "In Memory of Major Robert Gregory." There is the image of the drunken Lionel Johnson at a lodging-house table in Dublin and his clear, unshaken affirmation of faith, or of William Morris, now seen by Yeats as an embodiment of the "antithetical dream," or the rhetoric with which he puts Æ's political preoccupations in their place:

> Is it not certain that the Creator yawns in earthquake and thunder and other popular displays, but toils in rounding the delicate spiral of a shell?[1]

The autobiographies are full of such confident, dismissive, reverberating strokes, such literalising and bravura of metaphor; he seeks everywhere "correspondences," in Swedenborg's and Blake's sense, whereby a small fact or a minor personage is transformed into a symbol of mighty workings, a portion of a coherent, dramatised myth.

But the autobiographies are also full of evidence of Yeats's long striving for the condition of mastery in which he wrote them, the self-possession and power which finally enabled him to anneal emotion and thought in the greater poems. In revolt against the multiplicity of interest and opinion, the "many-headed foam," all that he attributed to Nature's sweet profusion, to her "winding path"—"Hodos Chameliontos," the way of the Chameleon, the region of disorder, where the artist is lost—he conceived the notion of "Unity of Culture defined and evoked by Unity of Image": but the uncontrollable flood of ideas, images, generalisations which this notion in its turn released swept him into further confusion:

> now image called up image in an endless procession, and I could not always choose among them with any confidence; and when I did choose, the image lost its intensity, or changed into some other image.[2]

The cultivation of a powerful syntax, the determination to impose patterns on experience by means of a philosophy of history sanctioned by private revelation, the discipline of the applied arts of the theatre—these were amongst the means that enabled Yeats to survive that dangerous, barren age, in which his "tragic generation" perished, between the death of Tennyson and the arrival of Ezra Pound in London. Powers of that kind contribute to the autobiographies and make it difficult to go behind them to a younger Yeats.

Nor, though there may be the need or desire to do so, is there much likelihood that it can be done. Every biographer who has any art at all, from Plutarch to Lytton Strachey, arranges his material in what Yeats called "stylistic arrangements of experience,"[3] and the autobiographies remain a chief source and an endless fascination. Almost all Yeats's earliest memories in *Reveries* are concerned with Sligo, where his mother's people, the Pollexfens, still lived, although it was in Dublin on 13 June 1865, that he was born, the first son of John Butler Yeats, a lawyer who was about to abandon the law for the profession of art. When this happened, in 1867, the family moved to London; and finally in 1876 they settled at the new "village" built by Norman Shaw, Bedford Park, Chiswick, a place which filled Yeats with romantic excitement because it was an escape from Victorian bad taste:

> The streets were not straight and dull . . . but wound about where there was a big tree or for the mere pleasure of winding, and there were wood palings instead of iron railings. . . . we only knew the most beautiful houses, the houses of artists.[4]

At Bedford Park people wore peacock-blue dresses and had peacock-blue doors; his father's friends were "painters who had been influenced by the Pre-Raphaelite movement but had lost their confidence." But it was

Sligo that counted most; many weeks were spent there every year in the house of his maternal grandfather William Pollexfen the "silent and fierce old man," who was in partnership with Yeats's grand-uncle William Middleton in the firm of Middleton and Pollexfen, millers and shipowners. Through Sligo Yeats reached back to the ancestors commemorated in the "Introductory Rhymes" to *Responsibilities* (1914): the Dublin linen-merchant Jervis Yeats (d. 1712); Benjamin Yeats (d. 1795), who by his marriage to Mary Butler united his line with a family of social distinction upon which the Yeatses always set great store; John Yeats, the Rector of Drumcliff five miles from Sligo; and his son, also a country rector, William Butler (1806–1862), the poet's grandfather, who constantly read Shelley and Lamb, and who married one of the Corbets, another Anglo-Irish family of some distinction. On the mother's side the Pollexfens had a reputation for substance and reserve; but the Yeatses were more talkative and less solid. The poet's father wrote of the Pollexfens' "curious solitariness," and of his own eagerness to communicate:

> when my son first revealed to me his gift of verse 'Ah!' I said, 'Behold I have given a tongue to the sea-cliffs'.[5]

The landscape of Sligo has remarkable variety and completeness: a sandy estuary and a harbour with stone quays, the steeply wooded slopes of Lough Gill descending into the islanded lake, lighthouse, ruined castles, the dark of the coppices and the cold light of the sea, all presided over to the north by the flat-topped Ben Bulben and to the south by the rounded Knock-na-Rea crowned by its enormous slag-heap of a cairn, beneath which Queen Maeve lies buried. Yeats tells of his adventures, fishing, yachting, and climbing, and of his delight in good local stories: but he was very often lonely and frightened, and did not believe in the happiness commonly attributed to childhood.

Yeats went (1875–80) to the Godolphin School at Hammersmith, where he learnt little, and was very conscious of the difference between other boys and himself, an Irishman and the son of an artist. In 1880 the family returned to Ireland and lived at Howth, Co. Dublin, while his father had a studio in the city, and the boy attended the Erasmus Smith High School (1880–3). His father's influence was paramount,[6] but he resisted his desire that he should go on to Trinity College, Dublin, and instead attended Art Schools in Dublin (1884–6). Since at least 1882 he had been writing poetry in imitation of Shelley and Spenser, and many verse plays with fantastic plots: his first lyrics were published in 1885; in the following year he abandoned the attempt to become a painter. The slow business of submitting poems and articles to periodicals began. The family returned to London in 1887 and finally settled again in Bedford Park.

In Ireland John O'Leary had helped him, and he had admired Edward Dowden's personality and Swinburnian verses, not then agreeing with his father's estimate of Dowden as a provincial professor who had sacrificed his creative gifts to the lectern and the intellect; at Dowden's house he met Katharine Tynan and Douglas Hyde for the first time, and he attended meetings of the Young Ireland Society, of which O'Leary was President; there were quarrels and rhetoric, especially from John F. Taylor, a great orator "imprisoned in himself," "the tragic figure of my youth,"[7] and "as a training for self-possession" Yeats himself made many speeches.

In London he was introduced to Morris and met Shaw and others at Kelmscott House suppers in Hammersmith. Bedford Park no longer possessed its old charm, "yet I was in all things Pre-Raphaelite";[8] Rossetti and Blake dominated (he had learnt about them from his father), and the little theatre at Bedford Park clubhouse stirred his imagination. He became one of W. E. Henley's "young men" and met Wilde at his house. *Four Years. 1887–1891*, the first section of *The Trembling of the Veil*, evokes all this life in London, and there are great, melancholy, yet ebullient portraits of Morris, Wilde, Henley, the symbolic painter J. T. Nettleship and others He was now getting literary work of various kinds, anthologising, writing for two American papers, even copying books in the Bodleian for publishers. The year 1889 was especially important: he published *The Wanderings of Oisin*; at Bedford Park he met Maud Gonne, Irish actress and revolutionary, for the first time, and started to write *The Countess Kathleen* for her; and he began work in collaboration with Edwin Ellis on an elaborate edition of Blake. His chief confidante in letters during this period was Katharine Tynan, the first of a series of notable women who played this role. These letters reveal that he had already defined his conception of Irish nationality and subject-matter in the context of his own self-criticism and sense of growth to come; John O'Leary had famously remarked that there are things a man must not do to save a nation, and Yeats might have added that one of them was writing bad, popular, patriotic poetry. These letters are less revealing about another preoccupation, his study of the occult. Yeats joined the Theosophical Society in 1890, and in the same year was initiated into the Order of the Golden Dawn, a society founded by MacGregor Mathers for the study and practice of magic. Symbols on pieces of cardboard were used to call up visions; the Order had an elaborate system of hierarchical grades borrowed from Rosicrucianism, and its name symbolised the rebirth of the adept and the regeneration of the world. The following year Yeats was one of the founding members of the London Irish Literary Society and of the Rhymers' Club. The Rhymers included Lionel Johnson, Ernest Dowson, John Davidson, Arthur Symons, and Victor Plarr, the original of Pound's "Monsieur Verog" in *Hugh Selwyn Mauberley*:

Mr. Yeats proposed that we should in future debate on poetry, and by way of beginning he made a speech, pointing out that poetry had at one time passed through four stages, which were, I think, the Diabolic, the Seraphic, the Celestial, and something else.[9]

But debates were voted out. Yeats later saw all the Rhymers as infected, in Ian Fletcher's phrase, with "the prophetic sickness of the solitary self-annihilator."[10] The Veil of the Temple was trembling; the Rhymers foresaw the destruction which must precede the Golden Dawn.

Such was multiplicity. Yeats dressed for the poetic role in long black cloak and flowing tie, and seemed to George Moore "an Irish parody of the poetry that I had seen all my life strutting its rhythmic way in the alleys of the Luxembourg Gardens." His days were further complicated by his love for Maud Gonne, probably the most important personal experience of his life. He first proposed marriage to her in 1891, and during 1892 was still hoping; she had been initiated into the Order of the Golden Dawn, and they attempted to share visions and symbols; many of the poems in *The Countess Kathleen and Various Legends and Lyrics* (1892) are addressed to her as the "Rose," symbol of eternal beauty. A liaison with the married woman whom he calls "Diana Vernon" interrupted but did not overcome this "barren passion" (1896), and during these years Yeats paid many visits to Paris where Maud Gonne was living; there were joint political activities, and in 1898 they entered into a mystical or spiritual marriage and searched for a means of communion of souls on the "astral plane." Yeats's despair is reflected in poems of this period. The final blow did not fall until Maud Gonne's marriage to John MacBride in June 1903, which "changed the look of things." Although he returned to "Diana Vernon," and there was a passionate interlude also with Florence Farr, the obsession with Maud Gonne was lasting. The "spiritual marriage" was renewed in 1908 after her separation from MacBride, and many poems up to 1916 and beyond are concerned with her. The last crisis came in 1916 after the execution of MacBride in the Easter Rising. Her final refusal ultimately determined his own marriage to Georgie Hyde-Lees in 1917. Yeats came to see Maud Gonne as a fated being, craving for something beyond the natural role that her beauty assigned to her, one who had bruised the body to pleasure soul, and for long she seemed to him to have frustrated his search for "Unity of Being" and cruelly sharpened his understanding of its supreme value. His own role as her courtly and Platonic lover was played out in pain and despair, and the poems that enact this role depend on the tension between praise of the sacred object and a relentless conviction about its nature.

In the period before 1900 Yeats established his habits of mind and the sources of his art. His career as a man of letters meanwhile proceeded apace. In Paris in 1894 he had attended a performance of Villiers de l'Isle Adam's *Axël*, which became the first of a succession of "Sacred Books." His interest in the theatre was growing all the time; his first meetings with both Lady Gregory and Synge occurred in 1896, and he grew better acquainted with George Moore. This was also the year in which he established himself at 18 Woburn Buildings, Bloomsbury, which was to be his London *pied à terre* for twenty years. He spent the summer of 1897—the first of many—at Lady Gregory's house, Coole Park, near Galway. He was ill from overwork and nervous strain, but the country life, Lady Gregory's order and calm, and the lakes and woods of the demesne which he so often wrote about restored his vitality. The plan for an Irish Literary Theatre was formed in these years, and the Antient Concert Rooms in Dublin saw a beginning in 1899 with the first performances of *The Countess Kathleen*. He col laborated with Moore on *Diarmuid and Grania* (performed in Dublin, 1901).[11] The Irish Literary Theatre was succeeded by a group of non-professional players, led by the brothers Frank and William Fay, which became the Irish National Theatre Company, with Yeats as President. Yeats began to collaborate with Lady Gregory in a series of one-act plays in prose. There was a quarrel with Moore over the play that became *Where There Is Nothing* (1902), and in the following year *In the Seven Woods*, which showed the influence of Coole Park, was the first book to be printed on the Dun Emer press established by Yeats's younger sister Elizabeth at what had now become, after their return to Dublin in 1902, the family house at Churchtown, Dundrum. The Abbey Theatre itself, which was given to the National Theatre Company by Miss Annie Horniman, did not open its doors until December 1904, and after its constitution had been settled in 1906, Yeats, Lady Gregory, and Synge were appointed its directors, an office which Yeats held for the rest of his life and which entailed the reading of manuscripts submitted for performance and endless concern with "theatre-business, management of men." Yeats was deeply implicated in all the crises of Abbey history, such as the row over Synge's *Playboy of the Western World* (1907). He also wrote much in defence of the theatre and in explanation of its principles; these writings were included as "The Irish Dramatic Movement" in the *Collected Works* which he now (in 1908) issued in eight volumes. The period after 1908 was not specially prolific, but was marked by the deliberate change in poetic style which characterises *The Green Helmet and Other Poems* (1910) and *Responsibilities* (1914).

There was also a revision of his ideas about the theatre. It was not a change of mind about his own work so much as a desire to free himself from what he conceived to be the Abbey's obligations to a popular, "objective" theatre. What happened was partly due to his association with Ezra Pound, whom he had first met in 1909, but did not get to know well until 1912. The years that culminated in the first play written in imitation of the Japanese Noh drama (1915) and the first volume of major achievement, *The Wild Swans at Coole* (1919), were exceptionally chaotic, various, and directly related to the verse: the Easter Rising; his final rejection by Maud Gonne; his marriage; the fortunes of Lady Gregory (her illness, the threat to her estate, the death of her son Robert); the acquisition of Thoor Ballylee (in April 1917), the Norman castle-tower not far from Coole which had been in his mind for years and now became the most substantial of his symbols; the birth of a daughter (1919), and of a son (1921). In addition, Yeats had for some time been systematising his philosophical mythology, which lies behind the plays of the second period (1915–38) and many of the poems.

In an essay which he wrote in 1914, and which was finally printed in Lady Gregory's *Visions and Beliefs in the West of Ireland*, he told how the dead communicate from out of their "earth-resembling" life with the living; his evidence came not only from Irish ghost-stories and the *séance*-room but also from the writings of Swedenborg and the Swedenborgians, the neo-Platonists, the Cambridge Platonists, and the Noh ghost plays. In *Per Amica Silentia Lunae* (written 1917), which, as a series of supercharged *pensées*, is the most successful book of its kind Yeats wrote, he sketches his doctrine of the self and the anti-self ("the Mask"), the notion that each man pursues in pain and desire ("the quarrel with ourselves") an opposing, imagined self, the reverse of that which operates in his ordinary, daily life. This is the burden of the *poète maudit*, who out of his cursed toil achieves a vision of antithetical beauty and momentary happiness. The roots of this idea lie far back in the symbolist doctrines which Yeats had learnt from Arthur Symons in the eighteen-nineties:

I find in an old diary: 'I think all happiness depends on
the energy to assume the mask of some other life, on a
re-birth as something not one's self, something created
in a moment and perpetually renewed. . . . If we cannot imagine ourselves as different from what we are,
and try to assume that second self, we cannot impose
a discipline upon ourselves. . . . Active virtue, as distinguished from the passive acceptance of a code, is
therefore theatrical, consciously dramatic, the wearing
of a mask. . . .[12]

These ideas had turned his work on *The Player Queen*
(begun in 1908) into confused allegory, but now they
were growing clearer. Finally, a few days after their
marriage, Mrs Yeats (who was exactly half Yeats's age
of fifty-two, and whom he had initiated into the Order of
the Golden Dawn in 1914) attempted automatic writing;
the messages which came excited him so much that he
began to construct the system which resulted in *A Vision*
(1925, and a much revised version in 1937). *A Vision* presents his philosophy of history, humankind, and life
after death. What the "Unknown Instructors" who
spoke through Mrs Yeats told him was a literalisation of
his own thoughts and beliefs: the classification of historical periods and of men and women according to a
scheme symbolised by the twenty-eight phases of the
moon, and the working of the *gyres* in history. History
becomes a system of antithetical movements diagram-
matised by the gyre, or spiral, traced round an imaginary
cone from apex to base; when the base is reached and the
gyre at its widest, the civilisation collapses in a violent
reversal and the new gyre begins again at the narrow
apex of the cone. In *A Vision*, also, he set out in detail and
with much technical language what happens to the
dead: the soul endures an elaborate purgatory in which
it purifies away in thought the events of its past life until
it is ready to be born again:

'Knowledge he shall unwind
Through victories of the mind,
Till, clambering at the cradle-side,
He dreams himself his mother's pride,
All knowledge lost in trance
Of sweeter ignorance.'[13]

The deterministic world of *A Vision* has no God, but
natural and supernatural interpenetrate; and men are
continually exposed to "shock" and "miracle." The
classification according to the phases of the moon was a
vast metaphor, "a stylistic arrangement of experience."
The point of it all was "getting one's mind into order"
and so allowing freedom to the impulse to create. Much
the most celebrated dictum of the unknown instructors
is: "We have come to give you metaphors for poetry."[14]

The exact relation of these metaphors to the plays and
poetry is the chief problem of Yeats criticism, and it re-
curs in later chapters. Two things are clear at this stage:
that the work for *A Vision*, whether it is the expression
or the cause of a new self-confidence, coincided with
the beginning of Yeats's greatest period; and that when
A Vision was completed, Yeats did not retreat into its
credal shell, but normally used it in the poetry and
plays only so far as the nature of his poetic and dramatic
kinds permitted. And since he had followed his nose for
the antithetical in constructing it out of antitheses, it is
not surprising that the whole system itself can be used as
a pose or gesture antithetical to the daily life of bewilderment and disorder, and that this larger dialogue is often
the subject-matter of his poetry. Yeats did not believe
that having found his mask, he was exempt from "new
bitterness, new disappointment" (in the contemplation
of the history of Ireland, for example, or of the "growing
murderousness of the world"), or suppose that he need
"never awake out of vision."[15] "One cannot be at
peace," he said, "in a country that is half made."

The tortured history of Ireland in rebellion and civil war filled Yeats's poetry. He lived now in Dublin and spent the summers at the Tower, where he wrote poetry most easily, and was a famous and diligent man of letters: Nobel prizewinner in 1923, Senator of the Irish Free State (1922-8). He was Chairman of the Senate Committee which was responsible for selecting the beautiful designs of birds and animals on the Irish coinage, but he did not accept re-election at the end of his term as Senator because of increasing ill health. Time was now spent abroad, in Spain, the Riviera, and a flat was found at Rapallo; it was not possible after 1929 to spend the summers in the damp and inconvenient Tower, and at Rapallo in 1930 he was seriously ill with Maltese fever. In the following year he went to see the stricken Lady Gregory, who died at Coole in 1932. He moved from Dublin to Riversdale, Rathfarnham, a house in the country with a garden. This was his last dwelling-place in Ireland. He had been reading a great deal of philosophy since the completion of the first edition of *A Vision* and corresponded much about it with T. Sturge Moore, the poet and brother of G. E. Moore, who had for long designed the covers of his books: his work, carefully carried out according to Yeatsian symbolism, may be seen on most of the volumes of lyrics and plays which comprise all Yeats's greatest writings: *The Wild Swans at Coole* (1919), *Michael Robartes and the Dancer* (1920, first printed, as were a majority of his books since 1903, on his sister's press, now called the Cuala Press), *Four Plays for Dancers* (1921), *The Tower* (1928), *The Winding Stair* (1933), *Wheels and Butterflies* (1934), *Last Poems and Plays* (1940). Yeats's history during his last years is in these and other writings rather than in the details of his movements. In 1934 he underwent the Steinach rejuvenation operation and thought that it had improved his health. He was full of excitement about poetry and politics, investigated the techniques of broadcasting poetry on the B.B.C., was even tempted to become a Professor in Japan, and seems to have enjoyed, in the compilation of the *Oxford Book of Modern Verse* (1936), making some other poets furious. A last friendship was with Dorothy Wellesley, the successor as correspondent and confidant to J. B. Yeats, John O'Leary, Katharine Tynan, Olivia Shakespear, Lady Gregory; he paid many visits to her Sussex home on his journeys between Ireland and the Continent (1935-8):

> Surely among a rich man's flowering lawns,
> Amid the rustle of his planted hills,
> Life overflows without ambitious pains. . . .[16]

Yeats survived the toils of ambition; "wildness" became a favourite word. There are many portraits and accounts of him in old age; Augustus John painted him full-faced and smiling, a very different image from the raven-haired, russet-browed "poet of the twilight," myopic, hieratic, whom John had drawn thirty years before.[17] Some photographs show a "wild old wicked man;" he wore blue and green now, not the inky cloak that had made George Moore compare him to an umbrella forgotten by a picnic party. At seventy he had, according to Stephen Spender, "something of the appearance of an overgrown art student, with shaggy hanging head and a dazed, grey, blind gaze."[18] Dorothy Wellesley noted his "small dark eyes turned outward . . . like those of a lizard"; "Under the lamp his hair seemed a pale sapphire blue. I thought while he talked 'What a beautiful man!' "[19] Did he wish to be revered? There was the self-mockery, the oafish life of the hero-fool—Congal, Cuchulain, the kitchen spit, the "foul rag-and-bone shop of the heart":

> Fifteen apparitions have I seen
> The worst a coat upon a coat-hanger. . . .

His health was very precarious, but his final illness

lasted only two or three days. He died at Cap Martin on the French Riviera on Saturday, 28 January 1939; two days before, he had been able to make corrections, and to alter the title of his testamentary poem from "His Convictions" to "Under Ben Bulben." After the War, in 1948, the Irish Government sent a corvette to bring his remains back home, and he was buried where John Yeats had once been Rector, in the Protestant Churchyard at Drumcliff, on the slope of the flat-topped mountain overlooking Sligo bay, as he had wished. In his last poem, the guardians of "The Black Tower" wait for the final dark of the moon to extinguish the age and listen for the sound of their lost king's great horn:

> *There in the tomb the dark grows blacker,*
> *But wind comes up from the shore:*
> *They shake when the winds roar,*
> *Old bones upon the mountain shake.*

REFERENCES

1. *A.*, p. 249.
2. *A.*, p. 270.
3. *V.* (1937), p. 25.
4. *A.*, p. 43.
5. J. B. Yeats, *Early Memories* (Cuala Press, Dublin, 1923), p. 20.
6. See especially *A.*, pp. 64–66.
7. *A.*, p. 98.
8. *A.*, p. 114.
9. Victor Plarr, *Ernest Dowson* (London, 1914), p. 63.
10. *Complete Poems of Ernest Dowson*, ed. I. Fletcher (London, 1953), p. xxxv.
11. See especially Moore, *Ave* (1933 edn.) pp. 264 ff.
12. *M.*, p. 334.
13. *C.P.*, p. 163.
14. *V.* (1937), p. 8.
15. *M.*, p. 342.
16. *C.P.*, p. 225.
17. Augustus John, *Chiaroscuro* (1962 edn.), p. 88; see also Gogarty, *It Isn't this Time of Year at All* (New York, 1954), p. 242.
18. S. Spender, *World within World* (London, 1951), p. 163.
19. *L.P.*, pp. 191, 213.

CHAPTER II

OISIN AND KATHLEEN

In 1889 Yeats issued nearly all of the verse which he had published up to that time in a small volume of 156 pages entitled *The Wanderings of Oisin and Other Poems*. It appeared in January, in the same month in which he had met Maud Gonne for the first time at his father's house at Bedford Park. Seventeen out of the thirty-one items in this volume, including the poetic play *Mosada* (1886) and *The Island of Statues* (1885), failed to gain admission to any other collection in Yeats's lifetime, although they can now be read in the "Variorum Edition." The seventy or so pages which are left include those famous and agreeable songs "Down By the Salley Gardens" and "To an Isle in the Water," but most of them are occupied by Yeats's first major attempt at an Irish mythological theme, the poem about Oisin. It still remains his longest poem, but was extensively revised before it was reprinted in *Poems* (1895).

Wilde praised the book in a review; Henley commended one of the poems in it; and when William Morris met the young author—he was twenty-four —in Holborn, he said "You write my sort of poetry," and "would have said more had he not caught sight of a new ornamental cast-iron lamp-post and got very heated upon that subject."[1] Yet, despite such formidable godfathers, *The Wanderings of Oisin* is a fairly rich and independent poem. It is written by a professional, not a literary boy, as *The Island of Statues* is. This is seen in Yeats's handling of his sources.[2] He knew no Gaelic and depended entirely upon translations, the chief one being Bryan O'Looney's version of "The Lay of Oisin in the Land of Youth" by Michael Comyn, a mid-eighteenth century Gaelic poet (though the legend of Oisin's three hundred years of dalliance with a super-natural being is of course much older). With this Yeats combined material from the Oisin-Patrick dialogues written in Middle Irish, and cleverly set the whole story within their framework: a narrative device that allows Oisin to tell his own story in the first person at a time when it is all over and Fenian might is withering before Christian truth. This gives the poem another dimension and increases its vitality. Although he was consciously acting as the successor of Sir Samuel Ferguson and other forgotten writers who had lately used Irish mythology, Yeats was not concerned simply to retell the Irish legends. The use of the "inherited subject-matter," the mythology, was not to be an educational device nor an aesthetic one, but something more deeply political— a deepening of the political passion of the nation by strengthening its imagination, by going back to the place where it is most itself and not any other country, the point where legend is born out of a culture at unity with itself, undistracted by the claim of other cultures or the abstract thought of the nineteenth century (whose art seemed to him to derive from a succession of inter-national, intellectual fashions):

I could not endure . . . an international art, picking stories and symbols where it pleased. Might I not, with health and good luck to aid me, create some new *Prometheus Unbound*; Patrick or Columcille, Oisin or Finn, in Prometheus' stead; and, instead of Caucasus, Cro-Patrick or Ben Bulben? Have not all races had their first unity from a mythology that marries them to rock and hill?[3]

Despite the influence of Shelley and Morris, such

thoughts helped Yeats to master his material, as well as to search for it and select it. He wrote to Katharine Tynan, shortly after the publication of *The Wanderings of Oisin*, that his ideas of a poem had changed greatly since *The Island of Statues*: " 'Oisin' is an incident or series of incidents; the 'Island of Statues' is a region." Once he had thought of a long poem as just such a region, into which one could wander from the cares of life as Morris did: "The characters were to be no more real than the shadows that people the Howth thicket. Their mission was to lessen the solitude without destroying its peace."⁴ The most striking feature of *The Wanderings of Oisin* is that, though it is concerned with the voyage of the hero to three Elysiums in each of which a single state of life is realised with the extreme of perfection and absoluteness that belongs only to the immortal world, there is a pervading restless movement and system of controlled antitheses which saves these shadowy places from the corruptions of languor and sameness. Yeats is well aware that "one of the great myths of the hero tells of his dissatisfaction with the 'Bowre of Bliss' and his willingness to return like Ulysses to the world of battle."⁵

The carefully-designed relationship of the three parts to each other accounts for this effect. A different rhyme-scheme and metre are used for each Book. Each island has, as it were, it own style, adapted to its own subject: the loose, rapid, dreamy joy of the Island of the Living, where they dance and sing and swoon with nectareous peace; the energy striving against the sombre oppression of the sea-palace where the hero fights the monster on the Island of Victories; and the long, closed movement of sleep. These contrasts are prevented from breaking up the poem into unrelated parts by what John Unterecker has described, in the best account of the poem, as "an internal structure of interrelated images . . . particularly images of bird and tree which are in turn supplemented by images of water and moon."⁶ These make it possible to read the poem "spatially," so that the blind eagles of Book II and the silent, flopping owls of Book III are stressed against the little, painted, singing, Asian birds of Book I. There are many other properties and incidents organised in this way; this organisation gives the lie to the opinion that the poem is "written almost entirely for the sake of the embroidery"[7] and that the story was chosen simply to allow Yeats a Morrisian holiday. That Yeats had learnt, perhaps from his own collation of Shelley's symbols,[8] to advance beyond Morris to the use of imagery which is structural as well as decorative, is most clearly seen in Book I, where the refrain of the immortals' song ("Nor the grey wandering osprey Sorrow") mediates the sensual music—the young in one another's arms—of this paradise. The bird of prey is destructive time; its force is strengthened by the descriptions elsewhere in the book of the storm of birds, which keep up a vividly-coloured harmony.[9] So Yeats introduces for the first time into his poetry the changeless bird of the Byzantium poems.

But Oisin himself is the poem's major metaphor and the place where we can best discern its antithetical life. His adventures have been very variously interpreted, and the way in which the three islands obviously represent different aspects of experience or three different kinds of life invites this. The first island is the land of youth and love, no country for old men; Yeats's feelings about Sligo and Innisfree entered into it. The second is a land of darkness and struggle, of a maturity somewhat histrionically prophesied; perhaps Yeats's feelings about his father, or about sexual desire, or about Ireland's struggle with England entered into it. The "demon dull and unsubduable," protean, sad, and disgusting, which occupies the abandoned palace of the sea-god Manannan, and which, after being slain, rises again every fourth day in an "endless war," is the first of Yeats's beasts of cyclical and recurrent destruction. This Book

seems particularly crowded with symbols still half-
Shelleyan and was the most difficult of the three to
write:

> I brought it round to my uncle George Pollexfen, and
> could hardly read, so collapsed I was. My voice quite
> broken. It really was a kind of vision. It beset me day
> and night.[10]

This suggests that the images of the second book really
did emerge from below the threshold of the conscious
mind and are perhaps predominantly sexual in origin.
But, as Yeats admitted, the second part, though it
dredges more deeply in this sense ("the most inspired,"
Yeats said), is also the least artistic of the three. The
episode of the maiden chained to eagles is weakly
elaborate in Shelley's manner; she vanishes from the
story inexplicably; although the description of the demon
and the fight is effective,[11] there is a lot of detail elsewhere
which is not better than Rider Haggard. The third book
has been seen as a parable of old age, or of the poet among
the thickets of Howth, in the "region" of dreams. This
book, which was the least rewritten of the three, owes
nothing to "The Lay of Oisin in the Land of Youth,"
but was derived from a free handling of various Irish
versions of the Seven Sleepers legend.[12] The long line
seems to help the poet to move easily into the final
episode, when Oisin returns to a Christian Ireland which
has destroyed the Fenian heroes: it expresses both the
murmurous and sleepy mood of the Island of Forgetfulness and the heroic challenge of the returning hero:
"Went the laughter of scorn from my mouth like the
roaring of wind in a wood."

Oisin's experience of these three contrasted islands does
not make the hero himself a rich character. The worlds
exist independently of him, states of perfection in which
he is primarily an intruder or an observer; if their meaning is deepened by attempts to transcribe their symbols

as youth and age, London or Ireland, sexuality or freedom
from desire, the process is one which leads us back, however uncertainly, to the poet himself and to the nature
and growth of *his* sensibility. Yet there is an element in the
poem, more centred on Oisin, which does show us Yeats
attempting to create a hero and a heroic dilemma,
separate from himself or at any rate partially objectified.
This element takes the form of an act of choosing, a
dialogue between the two halves of the soul. The
journey with Niamh is a journey out of time into an
immortal and otherworldly love, the "miraculeuse nuit
nuptiale" of Axël, *The Shadowy Waters* and some of the
later poems; Niamh in this aspect dominates Book I
(one of the awkwardnesses of the poem is that she often
seems *de trop* in later episodes); perhaps it was this part
that most pleased Morris, for, Douglas Bush reminds us,
"the thought of wandering hand in hand with a dream-
mistress (which is also a Shelleyan *summum bonum*) is recurrent in Morris."[13] But for Oisin this thought is also
a kind of exile; although all the islands compose a long
love-adventure, all become insipid in the end because he
longs for the real world of war and hunting and companions. This divided self is in its turn continuously
seen; the first-person form of the narrative and the
frequent irruption of St Patrick often turn the poem into
dialogue, at the places where the hero must reject and
choose again, be true to his domineering allegiance.
Although all this derives from a pattern fundamental to
the poet's own mind, it gives Oisin an inward, heroic
life; here he is truly the anvil on which the hammers beat,
not just a mediator; the man to whom the adventure
happened, not just the symbol of the poet's sensibility.
This is perhaps why the poem grows stronger in the
final lines, where Oisin discovers most signally his own
voice and identity in the instant of final decision and
becomes the first Yeatsian hero to choose nobly, and like
a fool:

Put the staff in my hands; for I go to the
            Fenians, O cleric, to chaunt
The war-songs that roused them of old; . . .[14]

Why did Yeats never write another long poem? The
reasons lie in the nature of contemporary poetry, but
The Wanderings of Oisin itself gives one or two clues. Its
construction is by means of planes of imagery and incidents that are left for the reader to fit together; though
this is acceptable as an elaborate type of narrative structure (nearer to Milton than to Morris), it is a system of
interlocking patterns which can be handled with
greater ease in the short poem: in the way in which, for
example, we read "Byzantium" and similar poems
"spatially," each stanza considered in relation to all the
others. Further, two *personae* struggle together in *The
Wanderings of Oisin*: the image-making poet who builds
Oisin's islands out of Irish mythology and Shelleyan
symbolism, and the emergent hero himself whose best
life is in dialogue, as St Patrick's interlocutor. Oisin is to
this extent a dramatic character in the making. It is not
surprising to find that the other major work of the period
is the intensely ambitious, though now much faded,
Countess Kathleen.

Yeats began to write the first version of this play in
1889 shortly after his first meeting with Maud Gonne.
The story of the Countess who sold her soul to the
demons in order to rescue her people from starvation had
been included in his folk-tale anthology the previous
year; he told John O'Leary that he had long been
thinking of making a play out of it. The play differs in
some important ways from its source. In the tale the
Countess's struggle is with the demon merchants, who
are aided by a wicked servant to rob her treasure-house
so that she can no longer help the poor. Although this
incident is retained in the play and does lead to the
Countess's final decision to sacrifice her soul, it is not

much stressed. Instead, Yeats invented another element with which to bestow personality upon the Countess, and his ends by giving her a kind of life which is hardly represented in the source at all. Her ultimate struggle is not with the demon merchants but with forces in her own being: the choice between, on the one hand, devoting all she has, her money, her compassion, and finally her soul, to the starving peasants, and, on the other, withdrawing into the world of dreams and imagination away from the evil of the time, from the "old worm o' the world" that frustrates her search for an inward, changeless peace.

In the course of thirty years Yeats revised the play many times, and the final version printed in *Poems* (1919) and in *Plays and Controversies* (1923) is very different from the one published in *The Countess Kathleen and Various Legends and Lyrics* in 1892. Perhaps the most interesting feature of this thirty years of rewriting is the way in which he expands and strengthens all the implications of his decision to make the Countess's choice one between the pagan world of Fenian dreams and the evil of times that demand her charity and succour. Yeats's method for developing this was vastly to enlarge the part of the poet Aleel (called Kevin in the 1892 version). New episodes were written in for him at each major revision, until eventually he has a part in each of the five scenes. He is the poet, dreamer, and lover who urges Kathleen's retirement to dreams and the Druid forest, to self-absorption and the subjective life of peaceful beauty, away from responsibilities and the objective life of self-sacrifice and war; he is wrought into a successful symbol (which has many links with Yeats's later verse) of the "unchristened heart," the messenger of Aedh and Angus. In the 1899 version Kathleen's need to choose is being embodied in this relationship to Aleel. Yeats can be observed learning the use of a theatrical strategy in order to make us alive to his pattern of counter-truths, which is now represented by two

dramatis personae. He ceases to depend so much upon a
protagonist too close in nature to the speaker of his
lyrics. But it is still true that the Countess's relation with
Aleel is never wholly realised. The Artist and the Saint
confront each other on the stage, but the Saint is moved
mostly to pity for the Artist; his story and his sorrow,
which she helps more and more to bring out, do not ever
become a genuine temptation which can weaken her
resolve by awakening a perilous compulsion in the depths
of her own nature. Thus, in choosing to substitute this
more personal vision for the conflict with demonic out-
rage which he found in his source, Yeats threw away one
theatrical opportunity without entirely mastering the
other. Although her longing is better defined by the
emergence of Aleel, as a dramatic character Kathleen
remains too disengaged.

This heroine makes a choice which is the opposite
of that made by Oisin, who prefers the Fenians to St
Patrick, the old heroic dream to the "grey Truth" of his
dwindled, withered, and prayerful world. This is one
sense in which the play itself is a "counter truth" to the
earlier poem. Yeats so described it nearly fifty years later
when he wrote "The Circus Animals' Desertion." But
even in 1892, in the preface to *The Countess Kathleen,* he
thought of them as opposites: *The Wanderings of Oisin* was
pre-Christian, had to do with vast and shadowy activities, and great impersonal emotions; *The Countess Kathleen*
is "an attempt to mingle personal thought and feeling
with the beliefs and customs of Christian Ireland."[1]
Although, as we have seen, there is much in *The Wanderings of Oisin* that seems to need explanation in terms of
"personal thought and feeling,"—so that the antithesis
will not wholly work—it is true that personal thought,
indeed autobiography, entered into *The Countess Kathleen*
and was one impulse which motivated the enlargement
of Aleel's part. Yeats, indeed, came to see the play
as have some of his later critics, as a transcription of

his relations with Maud Gonne, who so remarkably embodied the longings that had had to be satisfied with
Niamh:

> And then a counter-truth filled out its play,
> *The Countess Cathleen* was the name I gave it;
> She, pity-crazed, had given her soul away,
> But masterful Heaven had intervened to save it.
> I thought my dear must her own soul destroy,
> So did fanaticism and hate enslave it,[16]

Maud Gonne had been much present at the inception of
the play in the first months of 1889; for long Yeats tried
to persuade her to play the chief part on the stage; Aleel
becomes ever more plainly Yeats himself, the poet of the
Nineties, the author of "The Song of the Happy Shepherd," "The Two Trees," and *The Shadowy Waters*. But
the "pity-crazed" Countess of "The Circus Animals'
Desertion" is not recognisable as the Kathleen of the
play, whose final choice is not represented as an en-
slavement. It was only later that Yeats was able to see
the life of Maud Gonne as a parable about a woman who
betrays her own beauty by dedicating herself to an
"opinionated mind" and climbing on a wagonette to
scream.[17] The Countess is much more reverentially
handled; Yeats had as yet neither the excuse nor the style
to write so harshly of Maud Gonne.

Yeats's struggle as an artist with nationhood and
history begins in these works. Of nationhood more will
be said in the next chapter; but both *The Wanderings of
Oisin* and *The Countess Kathleen* were attempts to get
back beyond the Renaissance into a world of imaginative
unities, heroic or medieval. "There was something,"
he wrote at the end of his life, "in what I felt about
Deirdre, about Cuchulain, that rejected the Renaissance
and its characteristic metres."[18] Blank verse suited the
"vaguely medieval" *Kathleen* only when it was "almost
put out of joint," but then she was nearer history than

c

Oisin, who ends with the Homeric measure that seemed
more suitable for a heroic age. Medieval and heroic,
Christian and pre-Christian, blank verse and hexameter,
personal and impersonal emotion, Niamh the "faery
bride" and the actuality of Maud Gonne, and in the
centre of each work a choice to be made between subjectivity and objectivity, or the Fenian kingdom of images
and the world of St Patrick's spectres—these are the
crossways and counter-truths from amidst which Yeats
hoped to trace out "the only pathway from which he
may hope to see beauty and wisdom with his own eyes."[19]

REFERENCES

1. *A.*, p. 146.

2. See R. K. Alspach, "Some
   Sources of Yeats's *The
   Wanderings of Oisin,*'
   P.M.L.A. LVIII (1943),
   849–66.

3. *A.*, pp. 193–4.

4. *L.*, p. 106.

5. Hazard Adams, *Blake and
   Yeats* (Ithaca, 1954), p.
   148.

6. John Unterecker, *A Readers'
   Guide to W. B. Yeats*
   (London, 1959), pp. 49–
   50.

7. Dorothy M. Hoare, *The
   Works of Morris and of
   Yeats in Relation to Early
   Saga Literature* (Cambridge,
   1937), p. 114.

8. See below, p. 34

9. *C.P.*, p. 422.

10. *L.*, p. 87.

11. *C.P.*, pp. 428–9.

12. Alspach, *op. cit.*, pp. 862–
    865.

13. Douglas Bush, *Mythology
    and the Romantic Tradi-
    tion* (Cambridge, Mass.,
    1936), p. 312 n.

14. *C.P.*, pp. 445–47.

15. *The Countess Kathleen and
    Various Legends and Lyric,*
    (1892), pp. 7–8.

16. *C.P.*, pp. 391–2.

17. *C.P.*, pp. 213, 388.

18. *E. & I.*, p. 523.

19. Preface to *Poems* (1895),
    p. viii.

CHAPTER III

DISCOVERIES AND CONVICTIONS
1887–1903

> You must draw heaven and earth into your net.
> "The Poet of Ballyshannon."

The Wanderings of Oisin and *The Countess Kathleen* both derived from Yeats's decision, which was taken quite deliberately when he was about twenty, to make himself an Irish poet. He went to ancient mythology for *The Wanderings of Oisin* and to a supposedly Irish folk-tale for *The Countess Kathleen* and drew as well upon the same type of material for its immediate successor *The Land of Heart's Desire* (1894); these were the two principal sources at which the Irish imagination might strengthen itself by drinking at the fountains of its youth and the traditions kept alive amongst the people. In the reviews which he wrote for American journals between 1887 and 1892 he insisted that Irish writers must stick to Irish subject-matter—"We peer over the wall at our neighbor's instead of making our own garden fresh and beautiful";[1] and that they must get to know the literature of the imaginative periods of Irish history. When folk-tales and the speech of the Irish peasant are reported, the bad nineteenth-century tradition of steeping everything in a kind of stage Irish in order to gratify the expectations of the foreign reader must be abandoned. Yeats read very widely for his three anthologies of nineteenth-century Irish literature: *Fairy and Folk Tales of the Irish Peasantry* (1888), *Stories from Carleton* (1889), and *Representative Irish Tales* (1891). He found much to admire in a humour whose essence was dare-devilry and harum-scarum gentility and in the pathos and "gentle Arcadian beauty" of the folk-tales of Crofton Croker whose *Fairy Legends and Traditions* (1825) was the first of numerous later collections of folklore. But both the novelists and the folklorists were, in Yeats's view, injured by their narrow conception of Irish life; in Croker's hands, the *sidhe*, the gods of the earth, "dwindled to dancing mannikins";[2] in the works of Lover or Lever the stage Irishman is substituted for the serious passions and convictions of the true peasant; and even Carleton, the great novelist of Ireland, "like the animals in Milton, half-emerged from the earth and its brooding," was forced "to write for a class who wished to laugh a great deal, and who did not mind weeping a little, provided he allowed them always to keep their sense of superiority."[3]

Upon the anthologies ensued not only *Oisin* and *Kathleen* but Yeats's own collection of folklore *The Celtic Twilight* (1893, revised and enlarged 1902). Many literary currents, the work of the translators of mythological literature, of Standish O'Grady, Samuel Ferguson, Douglas Hyde, and the inspiration of the Fenian leader John O'Leary, with whom Yeats was very closely associated, flowed in favour of the movement to go down amongst the people and listen to what they had to say. But for Yeats, behind all this overt policy and exercising a deeper constraint, lay the landscape of his Sligo childhood and the country stories of the Middletons, the spirit at Rosses that looked like a flat-iron, and Mary Battle, his Sligo uncle's servant who had the second sight. "Much of my *Celtic Twilight* is but her daily speech."[4] Most of the pieces began as sketches for periodicals, and the book presents no grand design. But besides being a collection of folk-stories and superstitions it is a chapter of autobiography. Interwoven with these elements is a third: visionary meditation on the stories and places, so that we feel throughout the book the constant pressure of

Yeats's impulse to transcend his folk-tale material: "to show *in a vision* something of the face of Ireland."[5] It is not "systematical and learned," as Douglas Hyde's admired collection *Beside the Fire* (1891) had been, but "a handful of dreams":

> The voices melted into the twilight, and were mixed into the trees, and when I thought of the words they too melted away, and were mixed with the generations of men. Now it was a phrase, now it was an attitude of mind, an emotional form, that had carried my memory to older verses, or even to forgotten mythologies. I was carried so far that it was as though I came to one of the four rivers, and followed it under the wall of Paradise to the roots of the Trees of Knowledge and of Life.[6]

Three sections that follow upon one another may illustrate the method. "Village Ghosts" is a plain collection of little anecdotes, some with the sort of humour, some with that *frisson* that characterises Yeats's best stories of this sort, all told detachedly and inconclusively. "A Knight of the Sheep," its title suggested by Gerald Griffin's tale which had been included in *Representative Irish Tales*, is about Katharine Tynan's father the "strong farmer," and is a sliver from the nineteenth-century novelists' tradition.[7] In between these two, "Dust hath Closed Helen's Eye" presents the image that was made permanent in the second part of "The Tower," of Thoor Ballylee, Mary Hynes, and Raftery:

> Some few remembered still when I was young
> A peasant girl commended by a song,[8]

Here the old, poor, half-blind poet, the "handsomest girl in Ireland," and the landscape of Ballylee are linked with the mythology of Troy and wrought into a symbol of the "sorrow of beauty and of the magnificence and penury of dreams." Yeats begins with the remembered fragments of peasant talk and local wonder, the imaginative care for the past residing in humble description, and ascends from them, out of the "soil where all great art is rooted," into fable. "Dust hath Closed Helen's Eye" is written, as nearly twenty years later was *The Only Jealousy of Emer*, for "some country where all classes share in a half-mythological, half-philosophical folk-belief which the writer and his small audience lift into a new subtlety."[9] All his life Yeats longed for such a country. The principle at work in *The Celtic Twilight* and its companion-piece *The Land of Heart's Desire* is clearly stated in one of the earliest reviews:

> To the greater poets everything they see has its relation to the national life, and through them to the universal and divine life: nothing is an isolated artistic moment; there is a unity everywhere; everything fulfils a purpose that is not its own; the hailstone is a journeyman of God; the grass blade carries the universe upon its point. But to this universalism, this seeing of unity everywhere, you can only attain through what is near you, your nation, or, if you be no traveller, your village and the cobwebs on your walls.[10]

Yeats's quest for universalism dominates a series of major essays composed in the eighteen-nineties and collected together in *Ideas of Good and Evil* (1903) as well as the three volumes of *The Works of William Blake* (1893), done in collaboration with Edwin Ellis. The quest arose first from a sense of deprivation: the feeling that the unity of man and nature had burst into fragments and that reason, science, and the abstracting mind of the Anglo-Saxon had exiled human emotion from man's understanding of the universe. So he turns away from speculation and the "vegetable glass" of Nature, "where the heart withers," to the imagination as it is embodied in the words of the poets and in dreams and magical visions: "for I am certain that the imagination has some

way of lighting on the truth that the reason has not."[11]
For Yeats the finding of this way entails a search for the
"symbolic correspondences" which Swedenborg and
Blake had named and which make it intelligible to say
that "the hailstone is a journeyman of God," because
such a statement is a "seeing of unity"; it apprehends in
vision, in emotion and intellect conjoined, the divine
order of the whole universe. Wisdom of this kind speaks
first in symbols. These are not "isolated artistic moments," mere metaphors which do not carry any charge
of unfolding meanings, but "signs or representations of
any moral thing by the images or properties of natural
things" (Yeats accepts, with some reservations, the
dictionary definition, in his essay on "The Symbolism of
Poetry"). The symbol may be a hailstone, or a blade of
grass, or a grain of Irish sand; to contemplate it rightly
and lovingly, as the poet or mystic or visionary do, is
not to study the Blakean "vegetable glass" for its own
sake but to discover the shadow of imperishable things
and substances and to find the road into "some divine labyrinth."[12] Such symbols may be found also in the natural
world, in the poets, and in traditional objects of worship
and contemplation which also have stirred the intellect
and evoked the emotions of men throughout the ages:

> If I say 'white' or 'purple' in an ordinary line of poetry,
> they evoke emotions so exclusively that I cannot say
> why they move me; but if I bring them into the same
> sentence with such obvious intellectual symbols as a
> cross or a crown of thorns, I think of purity and
> sovereignty. . . . It is the intellect that decides where
> the reader shall ponder over the procession of the
> symbols, and if the symbols are merely emotional, he
> gazes from amid the accidents and destinies of the
> world; but if the symbols are intellectual too, he be-
> comes himself a part of pure intellect, and he is himself
> mingled with the procession. If I watch a rushy pool

in the moonlight, my emotion at its beauty is mixed with memories of the man that I have seen ploughing by its margin, or of the lovers I saw there a night ago; but if I look at the moon herself and remember any of her ancient names and meanings, I move among divine people, and things that have shaken off our mortality, the tower of ivory, the queen of waters, the shining stag among enchanted woods, the white hare sitting upon the hilltop, the fool of Faery with his shining cup full of dreams, and it may be 'make a friend of one of these images of wonder,' and 'meet the Lord in the air.' So, too, if one is moved by Shakespeare, who is content with emotional symbols that he may come the nearer to our sympathy, one is mixed with the whole spectacle of the world; while if one is moved by Dante, or by the myth of Demeter, one is mixed into the shadow of God or of a goddess. So, too, one is furthest from symbols when one is busy doing this or that, but the soul moves among symbols and unfolds in symbols when trance, or madness, or deep meditation has withdrawn it from every impulse but its own.[13]

Such a passage gives some notion of what Yeats meant when he spoke of the symbols as "an endlessly intermarrying family"; Dante or the mythological tale "cannot tell one thing without telling a hundred others"[14] (the principle is at work in *The Wanderings of Oisin*); for he agreed with Arthur Symons that symbolism is the "establishing of the links which hold the world together."[15] Like Hopkins's bluebell or De la Mare's snowdrop, such symbols or families of symbols ("the procession of the symbols") give Yeats news, if not of the creator God, then of the intricate harmony of the universe, a "divine labyrinth," which the imagination, itself become part of the family, both creates and receives when it is undistracted by business or reason and perhaps intensified by magical practices or ascetic disciplines. The symbols that carry furthest and multiply most vigorously in the mind with their own life are those that awaken both intellect and emotion. A symbol that is associated merely with an idea provides only a moment's amusement or leads straight to allegory, which is an operation of abstracting reason; a symbol that is purely emotional leaves us in the Keatsian sweetshop, the mere profusion and sweetness of nature, in the "sleep of nature where all is soft and melting," and tempts the artist away from the "labours of inspiration." But Nature, the delusive goddess, is, in Blakean phrase, a "net woven by Satan";[16] Yeats believes with Samuel Palmer, Blake's disciple, whom he was also studying at this time, that the soul must climb above her steepest summits, and that the artist must choose not to "see like a naturalist" but to see everything, even a man talking or gesturing,[17] as "expressive and symbolic . . . every form, every sound, every colour, every gesture, a signature of some unanalysable imaginative essence."[18] And so amongst the poets Yeats chooses not Shakespeare but Dante, not Morris, a worshipper of natural abundance, but Rossetti and Shelley, not Wordsworth but Blake; and he chooses occultism, not philosophy, as at once a source of symbols and a means of proving to himself the mind's capacity for "establishing the links."

The endlessly intermarrying families and the tales that tell a hundred things threaten to become a mere disorder in the mind, as bad as Nature's profusion: but "true Unity of Being, where all the nature murmurs in response if but a single note be touched, is found emotionally, instinctively, by the rejection of all experience not of the right quality, and by the limitation of its quantity." The getting of his mind into order was, Yeats told his father, the real impulse to create. It can be seen at work in the essay on "The Philosophy of Shelley's Poetry" and, on a much larger scale, in the

edition of Blake. In both we can observe his continual
acknowledgment of Blake's command to "set his symbols
in the great procession . . . in a certain order," suited to
his "imaginative energy."[19] He transformed into order
the poetry of Shelley, who was so often the victim, in
Yeats's own judgment, of rootless fantasy, by massing and
linking together Shelley's recurring images of wonder—
cave and fountain and tower—and so produced a world
which grew solid underfoot and consistent enough for the
soul's habitation. Some one scene, adventure or picture,
he says at the end of the essay on Shelley, can, if but
brooded over for a whole life, disentangle the soul;
perhaps this can only be properly done by the systematic
mystic, for the poet is caught up in the circumstances of
his art. Yet the mystic or occultist may help the poet to
transform his mind, too, into a burning-glass. Yeats would
have liked to be a seer as well as a poet; the dialogue
between them became his subject-matter.

Yeats's choice and limitation of symbols are illustrated
in the poems he wrote during the eighteen-nineties,
grouped in the section of *Collected Poems* entitled "The
Rose" and in the volume *The Wind Among the Reeds*
(1899).

Nature in these poems is symbolical, never described
for its own sake, and limited to the four elements or their
expression in woods, waves, winds or stars. The Irish
mythological figures, too, are dislimned into elemental
beings, spirits of the four elements. The chief relation
celebrated is that of the lover to his mistress and beyond
her or through her to a nature and a universe, which
constantly interconnect with or mirror his emotional
moods, his fears and desires, in their flame or flood, their
tides and clouds and trees. Because the theme is limited
in this way, and because of the severe restrictions on the
emblems and properties, including the diction, the two
collections achieve a general unity of tone, but at a price.
Earth, air, water, fire, their creatures, conjunctions and

oppositions are constantly interwoven through the poems, like the recurring patterns in an Indian carpet. Yeats handles them as arabesques, as though some tabu forbade him to represent the whole human image: pale waters, white stars, dim grey sea, white birds, burning hair, desolate winds, grey twilight, flaming West, pale dew, dim sand, cloud-pale eyelids. When these bits are put together into their pattern, in individual poems, or in the mind of the reader as he surveys the poems as a whole, nothing resembling a felt, natural or psychological landscape emerges: what we have instead is a demurely restricted language, of which the words are these symbols, and which, we apprehend, is being spoken by a rather shadowy *persona*. It is strange work to have come from a pupil of Blake, from those naked, sinewy bodies. Yeats uses his language of symbols, not for communicating but for crooning over in his head. He holds himself a little out of our reach, a priest at the altar, his back turned to us, invoking in ways that move him deeply but obscurely; and though he changes his name from Aedh to Hanrahan to Michael Robartes (here all aspects of the lover's imagination), the roles are played out in a dream, with closed eyes. When the Rose, the central symbol of the Order of the Golden Dawn (the Incorruptible Beauty, woman's beauty, the rose of peace, of battle, and in the poem called "The Secret Rose" the symbol of the coming change of all things), appears in the imagination, the posture of worship is more extreme, for this is a secret symbol unlike the more traditional four elements: but the voice, though its volume rises, is still a voice in the head. It is their rhythmic beauty, their wavering enchantment of line, and their modesty of proportion, a keeping of scale, that makes these poems professional; it is *that* kind of seriousness which now appears as a specific symptom of poetic power—a matter of decorum and of rhetoric, coupled with inborn rhythmic sense.

This half-silent, tapestry-like verse sets the standard
from which one or two poems in the "Rose" section
depart—notably "The Man who Dreamed of Fairy-
land," with its firm structure, its objectification of the
character described, and even in its earliest version, its
unsleepy lines ("that cold and vapour-turbaned steep").
"The Two Trees," a poem about Maud Gonne, the
Tree of Life and Imagination, and the Tree of Knowledge and Death, by its directness of address and its
splendidly articulated cabbalistic and Blakean symbolism does build an "image of wonder." It is because on
this occasion we see and participate in the building process that "The Two Trees" draws us in with its own
energies. Also, in the way in which it handles in verse
what was to become a dominant idea the poem is a
prophetic one. In this case the idea is that a beautiful
woman should not despoil the subjectivity of her nature
by the politics of objectivity, or sacrifice the unity of her
being to a cause outside itself; this subject is antici-
pated in *The Countess Kathleen* and fully presented in
such later poems as "A Prayer for my Daughter" and
"In Memory of Eva Gore-Booth and Con Markiewicz."

The place of ideas of this kind in Yeats's work is worth
trying to define here, because so many of them were
formed before the turn of the century, and remained with
him always. He tells us in *The Trembling of the Veil* that he
was ashamed of the way in which generalisations flooded
his mind in his twenties; he could not "choose from
among them those that belonged to my life,"[20] and
would not permit them into his poetry because they arose
from the "intellect which I considered impure";[21] as a
result the poetry turned sentimental. But:

As life goes on we discover that certain thoughts sustain us in defeat, or give us victory, whether over ourselves or others, and it is these thoughts, tested by
passion, that we call convictions. Among subjective

men (in all those, that is, who must spin a web out of their own bowels) the victory is an intellectual daily re-creation of all that exterior fate snatches away. . .[22]

The "conviction" is a personal discovery, accepted upon an inward authority, and "tested by passion." Poetry, Yeats discovered, which excludes the intellect becomes sentimental, empty and fantastic; poetry cannot be separated from philosophy and belief, but it can incorporate them by portraying "the emotions of a soul dwelling in the presence of certain ideas." Richard Ellmann, who has provided a valuable account of this matter in the third chapter of his *Identity of Yeats*, has summed it up in the phrase "Assertion without Doctrine"; he describes Yeats's finally matured practice in this way:

> The poem may use beliefs, but must never seem to have been written merely to express them. They must be fused, along with emotional and formal patterns, into a unit with its own autonomy, where their function as beliefs is lost or unimportant. . . . Before he was thirty Yeats framed his principle of including statements in his verse without implying that they had any validity outside the particular poem in which they appeared . . . . Ideas, like nature and the passions, furnish the poet with material, and his task is to weld them into poems. Ideas which are true are those which lend themselves to this treatment. Ideas which are false or insincere remain isolated abstractions and spoil the poem;[23]

A list of Yeats's "convictions" divorced from the poetry, even if they were largely formed as "generalisations" before most of the poetry incorporating them was written, is therefore likely to be misleading. It is even more dangerous to use the poems merely as ciphers for decoding the generalisations. But it is a fact of the bio-

graphy, which can be discovered from the prose-writings
of the eighteen-nineties and from the retrospective
accounts of the period in the *Autobiographies*, that many
of the thoughts were shaped in these years, and only
needed separation from momentary opinions and the
testing of their value by time and passion to become
convictions and to be used as assertions in the later verse
—for in this context, time *is* passion: an idea held for
long enough becomes a portion of the affective self.

The "necessity for symbolism" was such a thought, as
was the decorum of the Irish setting; both of them
closely connected with a third: the conviction that the
"world was now but a bundle of fragments" and that the
enemy of its lost and desired unity of being, in the individual, the nation, and the arts, was abstraction, that
seeks to cage the "yellow-eyed hawk of the mind" and
destroy the absorption in a unifying image. From magical
and theosophical studies, and from such "sacred books"
as Villiers de L'Isle Adam's *Axël* Yeats took many other
generalisations; he is not often so frankly credal in expressing them as when he describes his belief in the
"great memory" in the first paragraph of the essay on
"Magic" (1901); for, just as Yeats, as Ellmann puts it,
"relies on the complexity of poetic structure to prevent his
verse from becoming doctrinal"[24] so he relies on a powerfully rhythmical and metaphorical prose-style and an
oracular rather than dialectical handling of the themes
to prevent his essays or stories ceasing to be primarily
works of art. Yet in these writings can be traced many
later poetic "assertions" and "convictions." Two of the
most important are the notion of a coming change in
the world, signalised by Mallarmé's phrase about
the "trembling of the veil of the Temple" before it
is rent in interlocking catastrophe and revelation, and
of rebirth and its counterpart, the hope of escape from
the round of incarnations into a changeless and immortal
existence.

The first idea enters into several of the stories in *The Adoration of the Magi* and *The Secret Rose* (1897), volumes which, as Giorgio Melchiori has shown, ought not to be neglected by anyone concerned to understand the origins of "The Second Coming" (1920) or "Leda and the Swan" (1924), not to mention such plays as *The Player Queen* (1922) and *The Resurrection* (1931). Yeats used the theme at the same time in "The Valley of the Black Pig" (1896), but it is characteristic of his attitude to his poetry at this time that the long note he wrote for this poem in *The Wind Among the Reeds*[25] is much more lovingly explicit about its subject than the vague little lyric. Comparatively explicit, too, is "The Adoration of the Magi", where the new magi are summoned from the west of Ireland to the bedside of a dying prostitute in Paris to learn from her the secret names of the returning gods. When Yeats revised the story for publication in 1925 the prostitute has become more explicitly still the harlot of the new annunciation,[26] another Leda, but even in its first version Virgil's prophecy of the cyclical return of civilisations is present in anticipation of the song in *The Resurrection*.[27] In the speech given, after the harlot's death, to the old woman who has been attending her—a speech full of scepticism and bewilderment—we can see Yeats's willingness to make even this portentous material, in which his imagination and intellect were so deeply engaged, part of a dramatic scene.[28] This principle is of the utmost importance for the understanding of how Yeats uses his ideas in his best plays and poetry, as expressions of the ideas of the *personae*, rather than as doctrines demanding the reader's assent. The alchemical stories "Rosa Alchemica" and "The Tables of the Law" obey the principle perhaps most obviously by being, frankly, stories. The narrator in "Rosa Alchemica," dissatisfied in the midst of a life modelled on that of Des Esseintes, restless for the final wisdom amongst his preciously garnered symbols, is, in the manner of some prototypical Synge, mesmerised by the alchemical initiate Michael Robartes into travelling (by train and boat) to the west of Ireland, of all places, in order to learn truth by alchemical ritual. But he ends by fleeing in disorder from the Temple of the Alchemical Rose, and thenceforth carries the rosary about his neck and a heart divided between the terror and the fascination of what may be only "the illusions that creep like maggots into civilisations when they begin to decline, and into minds when they begin to decay."[29] Similarly in "The Tables of the Law" (Aherne and another devout, but disturbed, narrator are the persons) a dramatic dialectic is made out of the conflict between old orthodoxy, whose prophet is Jesus, and the new revelation, whose prophets include Joachim of Flora, Jonathan Swift and the Pre-Raphaelites. And these safely dramatised stories were written not long after a period when Yeats was causing concern to his father and his friends by what seemed too intense and total an absorption in the mysterious affairs of the Order of the Golden Dawn.

But they need not have worried. Yeats was already convinced that "picture and dramatization" were his primary concern; he was an artist first and last and never lost his pleasure and pride in being one. From beginning to end this shines through the great collection of his letters: to write, to print, to revise, to be a *man of letters*— Yeats never seriously lost his zest for the role, as had some other great romantics before him. Much in his early work both as it succeeded and failed—the failure or absence of the *persona* in the early poems, the invention of the characters in the stories and of the elaborate stylist who wrote the essays, the faintly emergent protagonists of *The Wanderings of Oisin* and *The Countess Kathleen*— point straight towards the literal interpretation of his concern for picture and dramatisation as a need for the theatre itself, for characterisation and for "stage-picture":

Among the things that dramatic action must burn up are the author's opinions; while he is writing he has no business to know anything that is not a portion of that action.[30]

REFERENCES

1. *Letters to the New Island*, p. 106.

2. *Representative Irish Tales*, First Series, p. 5.

3. *Stories from Carleton*, p. xvii, *Representative Irish Tales*, First Series, p. 9. Thomas Flanagan's excellent book *The Irish Novelists 1800–1850* (New York, 1959) pays tribute to Yeats's understanding of the subject.

4. *A.*, p. 71.

5. *C.W.*, V. 1.

6. *M.*, p. 138.

7. Katherine Tynan tells the same story in her *Twenty-Five Years* (1913), pp. 7–8

8. *C.P.*, p. 219.

9. *F.P.D.*, p. 106.

10. *Letters to the New Island*, p. 174.

11. *E. & I.*, p. 65.

12. *E. & I.*, p. 117.

13. *E. & I.*, pp. 161–62.

14. *The Works of William Blake*, I. 282–83.

15. A. Symons, *The Symbolist Movement in Literature* (1899), p. 146.

16. *E. & I.*, p. 132.

17. *The Works of William Blake* I. 239.

18. A. H. Palmer, *The Life and Letters of Samuel Palmer* (1892), p. 43.

19. *E. & I.*, pp. 149–50.

20. *A.*, p. 83.

21. *A.*, p. 188.

22. *A.*, p. 189.

23. R. Ellmann, *The Identity of Yeats* (London, 1954), pp. 40 ff.

24. *Op. cit.*, p. 55.

25. *The Wind Among the Reeds* (1899), pp. 95–102.

26. *M.*, p. 312.

27. *C.W.*, VII. 170; *C. Plays*, p. 580.

28. *C.W.*, VII. 176.

29. *C.W.*, VII. 117.

30. *L.*, p. 741.

CHAPTER IV

THE PLAYS: FIRST PERIOD 1900–14

The three most important and interesting plays of this period are *The King's Threshold*, *Deirdre*, and *On Baile's Strand*. They share a common theme, the conflict between an objective world of established values, of government, concord, and reason, and the passion of the hero, which affirms the inward self and all the wasteful virtues. In *The King's Threshold* Seanchan the poet gives up his life in a prophetic ecstasy rather than yield to King Guaire's demand that poetry should accept its banishment from the council table. In *On Baile's Strand* Cuchulain the free warrior clashes with the High King of Ireland but, by betraying his own nature, becomes the victim of an evil will outside himself. In *Deirdre* the heroine triumphs finally, in a great act of the loving imagination, over her own weakness and over the possessive bonds of King Conchubar's amorous will. This conflict is of the same kind that came much more faintly to life between the subjective poetic world of Aleel in *The Countess Kathleen* and the demands made upon the heroine by the suffering of the actual world about her, and between Forgael's dream and his companions' greed and common sense in *The Shadowy Waters*. Yeats had appeared to choose Aleel's and Forgael's world, which is the world of *The Rose* and *The Wind Among the Reeds*; but all his art, as he came to discover, perhaps chiefly in the process of writing these plays, was to be essentially a dialogue between objective and subjective. In the plays the objective world is at last wrought explicitly into the structure and, since its place is recognised within the work of art, the true dramatic encounter becomes possible. All the plays are tragedies, and for Yeats tragic art is, above all, passionate art. He defines passion as "the straining of man's being against some obstacle that obstructs its unity."[1] A passion can only be contemplated in a work of art "when separated by itself, purified of all but itself, and aroused into a perfect intensity by opposition with some other passion, or it may be with the law."[2] Tragedy, he thought, unlike comedy, tends not towards the definition and discrimination of individuality, to all that is called character, but towards those moments when individuality sinks away, when drama is "emptied" of the naïvely human:

amid the great moments, when Timon orders his tomb, when Hamlet cries to Horatio 'absent thee from felicity awhile,' when Anthony names 'Of many thousand kisses the poor last,' all is lyricism, unmixed passion, 'the integrity of fire.'[3]

It is this "ritual of passion" that induces in the audience the condition of "tragic reverie," a condition which is easily disturbed by an awkward gesture or a misplaced stage-effect, and which is frustrated by the trappings of the naturalistic theatre, by hysteria, elocutionary expertise or constantly varying attitudes on the actor's part. Yeats's theatre values stillness, and stresses the distinguished, solitary, and proud; he wanted his actors to look more and more like Byzantine icons, and finally covered the tawdry human face with a mask. There remained for them only the energy and precision of subtle speech, which arises from the depth of the soul and so communicates with the soul of the audience; for in the moments of tragic reverie audience and performer draw upon the *anima mundi*, "that soul which is alike in all men," and startle us with our own secret thoughts.[4]

The King's Threshold (produced 8 Oct. 1903), the least impressive of the three plays, presents well enough the dialogue between the objective and subjective worlds and moves through it towards a "ritual of passion." The sense of locality is strong and the temptations offered to Seanchan to break his fast are solidly realised; his different visitors, the Mayor of Kinvara, the soldier, the monk, the chamberlain, the cripples bring with them a circumstantial world of provincial pride, sick cattle, and salt fish, and they quarrel convincingly. The episodes are organised in "Greek" fashion, as Yeats himself said,[5] round the poetic Samson, Seanchan; he is an obdurate professional, not a dreamer like Aleel. As he is separated and purified from everything, his mind rises out of delirium and weakness into the intensity of prophecy, into "joy," and he assumes the role of the "man that dies," with a vision, like that of Paul Ruttledge in *Where There Is Nothing*, of the future race that lies beyond the world of death. The symbols that mediate this antithesis—the infected moon, and the joyful, pro-creative stars—because they are located in dramatic speech, and because the speaker has a situation and a history, come to us with the passion and directness that was lacking in the symbolic language of the earlier lyrics. But it is precisely the "absolute and uncontaminated" nature of Seanchan's poetic faith, as Una Ellis-Fermor describes it,[6] that makes the play difficult to accept now; although Seanchan's message of rejoicing is the same as the one which came to the old man by the cave that's christened Alt,[7] his character and the faith which he holds are finally so purified of irony and compromise that they lack salt. Yeats still exempts the "ritual of passion" itself from the sardonic eye that was to turn even poets into old scarecrows.

Deirdre (produced 24 Nov. 1906) has a different structure. We are told at the beginning of the play, by the authority of the Musicians, whose skill in reading omens and whose experience as storytellers inform them what kind of story they are in, that the tale is to have a tragic ending; that Deirdre is trapped and that Conchubar is determined to kill her lover Naoise and possess her. When Deirdre enters, we watch her gradually finding out the nature of the story she is in; her understanding is stressed against the foolish hopes and mistakings of Naoise and Fergus. Her imaginative effort becomes directed to altering the story from within by the assumption of a series of roles; she tries to pretend that after all she does not love Naoise so that he may escape, then to await death in the posture of an ancient heroine, a role which in its turn breaks down when she pleads with Conchubar for Naoise's life, and finally, after Naoise is killed, she plays her most testing part and wrenches the story towards the end she now designs for it: she assumes the role of a half-reluctant mistress, attracted by Conchubar and yet angry with him because he will not allow her a moment to adjust herself to her new dignity by brief mourning over her former lover's corpse. Conchubar is convinced and unknowingly allows her time to die behind the curtain upon the body of Naoise. She finishes the story in her way, and not Conchubar's, by a great effort of the imagination and will, by a climactic disguising. That is the form *her* "ritual of passion" takes. This is a remarkable and successful scheme, and does have the effect of making us live with the character as she creates her conscious paradigm of roles. Deirdre stands out from her background as no Yeatsian character hitherto has done. For this reason, it is difficult to admit that Yeats has emptied his play of character, in the ordinary sense, although it is true that, if we can share in Deirdre's efforts to see her life in her way and not another's, what separates her from us may melt away in that movement of tragic sympathy which Yeats called "a drowning and breaking of the dykes that separate man from man."[8]

On Baile's Strand (produced 27 Dec. 1904) is a more complex and ambitious achievement than either of the other two. It is the first of what turned out to be five plays about Cuchulain. In the collected edition Yeats preceded it by *The Golden Helmet* (1908), rewritten as *The Green Helmet* (1910), which is a play that most shows Cuchulain, in Yeats's phrase, as "creative joy separated from fear."[9] In *The Golden Helmet* the champion turns out not to be the mightiest but the most comely-hearted, the one who wishes to transform discord into harmony by turning the coveted prize, the golden helmet, into a drinking-cup to be shared by all. The hero of *On Baile's Strand* is a more troubled figure. Unlike Deirdre and Seanchan, he is not single-hearted in his opposition to the objective world of order, represented by King Conchubar, but also, more specifically, by fixed values of inheritance and kinship: Conchubar has sons who will succeed him, Cuchulain has none, and his childless condition is a dangerous emblem of the old, untamed, heroic self. Begotten by a god, he glories in this turbulence; but Conchubar knows that in his sleep Cuchulain cries out despairingly "I have no son." This division of the hero's self against itself is the weakness at which, when the play begins, Conchubar is levering in his endeavour to get Cuchulain to swear an oath of obedience to him. For the play is about how the building of a city and a kingdom destroys another kind of life. Conchubar, planning his kingdom, wants to establish it upon the union of Cuchulain's warrior-strength with his own wisdom; his most powerful argument is that Cuchulain, hunting and dancing with his wild companions, has left the shore unguarded so that an unknown warrior from Scotland has been able to land. (This interweaving of the themes into the initiation of the main action is particularly skilful and was achieved only after the first half of the play performed in 1904 had been entirely rewritten). Cuchulain, weakened, finally gives way and takes the oath; it is an oath specifically directed against the power of the shape-changing witches and the wild, antithetical hate and love—"the brief forgiveness between opposites"—which had bound together Aoife and Cuchulain long ago in Scotland; by taking it, Cuchulain repudiates the golden liberty, which has been his joy and his secret despair. The oath is no sooner done than the unknown warrior from Scotland, Conlaoch, arrives with his challenge to Cuchulain. Struck by his resemblance to Aoife, which answers to his deepest wish for a son, Cuchulain wants to make a comrade of him; but this is the first test of his new allegiance and of the kingdom's power to defend itself against intruders, and Conchubar insists upon the fight. In a fury of sudden movement, when Cuchulain strikes the High King, he is persuaded that Conlaoch's power over him is the power of witchcraft again at work, and they rush to their swords. So Cuchulain kills his own son, as he learns at the end of the play from the Fool and from the Blind Man, who knows everything.

The hero's destiny and character are here trapped in a network of ironies, as are King Conchubar's. Both, when they least suppose it to be so, are in the power of Aoife's witchcraft and evil will—Conchubar when he insists on ruining what was to be the strength that upheld the stability of his land, Cuchulain when he fights the son whom the new movement towards peace and kinship, intensified in him by the oath that repudiates wildness, presents to him in a form that answers to his wish. But it cannot be fully recognised because he is made foolish by the new allegiance. That Cuchulain and Conchubar are playing the roles of blind man and fool is of course brought home by the presence of Blind Man and Fool at the beginning and end of the play; they are cleverly used, not only as expositors and as possessors of the secret that drives Cuchulain mad, but also as a means of enforcing the main theme of foolish strength entangled with dependent wisdom and of framing all this heroic circumstance within a sardonic commentary from common life: what is the death of heroes, and all that fuss and fury, beside a chicken in the pot? In *On Baile's Strand* Yeats at last works out his strategy for depicting the mythological hero, that of building episode against episode and character against character in an ironic order. This is to be the method used in all the plays, but most obviously in the plays about Cuchulain and in *The Herne's Egg*. But though the hero turns out to be a kind of fool, Yeats only salted his heroism with his foolishness and did not allow us to look upon him with a rancorous eye or "pull established honour down."

Yet *On Baile's Strand* does not fit Yeats's theory of tragedy, if only because the exclusion or lessening of character occurs even less in this play than in *Deirdre*. The very success of the Abbey made Yeats frightened of the theatre and awakened old suspicions of its power to move us not with the *anima mundi*, not with "life," but with excitements and energies that are specialised within the theatre itself "before the footlights":[10]

> Players and painted stage took all my love,
> And not those things that they were emblems of.[11]

For long he struggled to write a play of ideas—*The Player Queen* was begun in 1908—which might be a means of putting theatrical artifice in its proper, subordinate place: but the ideas domineered instead of creating order, and *The Player Queen* had to be laid aside. When he resumed writing for the theatre after a long interval these old quarrels broke out afresh.

REFERENCES

1. *E.*, p. 252.
2. *E.*, p. 155.
3. *E. & I.*, p. 240.
4. *A.*, p. 471; *E.*, p. 144.
5. *L.*, p. 409.
6. Ellis-Fermor, *The Irish Dramatic Movement* (London, 1954 edn.), p. 94.
7. "The Man and the Echo," *C.P.* p. 394.
8. *E. & I.*, p. 241.
9. *L.*, p. 913.
10. *E.*, p. 213.
11. *C.P.*, p. 392.

CHAPTER V

THE POEMS
1904–33

All that is personal soon rots; it must be
packed in ice or salt.
"A General Introduction to my Work"

Yeats's poetry, like Milton's, passes from decorative beauty through eloquence and magniloquence to a condition beyond eloquence—not to Milton's austere witnessing, but almost to song, spare and high and free. Thereafter, in the final phase, it maintains an equilibrium, magniloquent at times, at times stripped and singing. The poem that he wrote for his death, "Under Ben Bulben", encloses in varying panels of exhortation a three-line epitaph designed to be cut on stone. As a whole, and in almost all its parts, the development inspires awe.

In his plays up to this time Yeats had not achieved that kind of eloquence. Except in the prose-passages, where the influence of Lady Gregory must be allowed for, the style is a borrowed style, blank verse too reminiscent of the rhythms of Jacobean drama. All the characters in *Deirdre*, for example, speak in the same grave, rather careful, way, and the carefulness devolves upon them not from any inward movement of character but externally from Yeats's anxiety to make their speech refined and simple. So their grammar has an unnatural perfection and they seem to be assiduously observing the laws of punctuation when they should be following the dictates of the heart:

DEIRDRE: Why should you die? I will not live long,
Naoise.
    I'd not have you believe I'd long stay living;
    O no, no, no! You will go far away.
    You will forget me. Speak, speak, Naoise, speak,
    And say that it is better that I go.
    I will not ask it. Do not speak a word,
    For I will take it all upon myself.
    Conchubar, I will go.

NAOISE: And do you think
    That, were I given life at such a price,
    I would not cast it from me? O my eagle!
    Why do you beat vain wings upon the rock
    When hollow night's above?[1]

For sudden surges and expansions of feeling Yeats relies on metaphor, on language suddenly turned "poetic" in the midst of the simplicity, with no corresponding shudder in the rhythm; even the cries are fitted into the dominant rhythmic pattern, and the elisions that seem colloquial are really there because the dramatist is making an iambic pentameter. The conscious simplicity and noble pathos of the characters—Deirdre's "For what am I, to be remembered always?", Seanchan's "Child, child, I must not eat it though I die"—emerge in lines of careful memorability which detach us from the persons by putting us in mind of the playwright; he is manoeuvring them into the position for pure and fine utterance of this kind, and therefore it fails to be fully effective. In recognising that dramatic action must burn up the author's opinions, Yeats did not attain the further recognition that it must, in another sense, burn up his opinion of himself as a poet too.

Yet it seems certain that it was the playwright's readiness to submit to the obligation to dramatise personalities that changed the character of Yeats's lyric verse, and made that dramatic, too. By discovering character in others, he discovered character in himself, and puts himself into his verse as a *dramatis persona*. This entailed a repudiation of the "decorative landscape and still life," of the "impersonal beauty", of the earlier poems:

> I was interested in nothing but states of mind, lyrical moments, intellectual essences. . . . I had not learned what sweetness, what rhythmic movement, there is in those who have become the joy that is themselves. Without knowing it, I had come to care for nothing but impersonal beauty. . . . Then one day I understood quite suddenly, as the way is, that I was seeking something unchanging and unmixed and always outside myself, a Stone or an Elixir that was always out of reach, and that I myself was the fleeting thing that held out its hand. . . . Presently I found that I entered into myself and pictured myself and not some essence when I was not seeking beauty at all, but merely to lighten the mind of some burden of love or bitterness thrown upon it by the events of life. . . . To put it otherwise, we should ascend out of common interests, the thoughts of the newspapers, of the market-place, of men of science, but only so far as we can carry the normal, passionate, reasoning self, the personality as a whole.[2]

"To dramatize myself," and to "express not the traditional poet, but . . . the normal active man"[3] became his ambition: but this did not mean that symbolism was forsaken, only that the poem did not present the symbols without context, but contained both the man and his symbols, arranged in an effective order—the Stone or the Elixir, and the "I myself" who holds out his hand to them.

It is the establishment of contact with the *personae* and their speech that makes possible "Adam's Curse," the most significant, if not the most flawless, poem in the 1904 collection *In the Seven Woods*, Yeats's first volume of new poetry since *The Wind among the Reeds*. "Adam's Curse" is a conversation-poem between three people,

and the conversation has a force, perhaps chiefly aided
by the rhyme, that is not often found in the plays themselves. It is not entirely successful:

> 'Better go down upon your marrow-bones
> And scrub a kitchen-pavement, or break stones
> Like an old pauper, in all kinds of weather;
> For to articulate sweet sounds together
> Is to work harder than all these, and yet
> Be thought an idler by the noisy set
> Of bankers, schoolmasters, and clergymen
> The martyrs call the world.'[4]

The third line has a vitally repeated pattern of indignant
feeling—páuper/wéather, but the last four lines go
wrong, seem lexically tame, and are too anxiously
crammed up to make the measure and to finish the
sentence; the stresses go awry in the penultimate line—
the natural speech-stress frustrated by the metrical one,
with the result that words such as "banker" or "clergy-
man" appear self-conscious intruders. In the next
section, too, there is an attempt to enlarge the status and
associations of the speaker in a way that appears too
great for the necessarily parenthetical position of the
sentiment: for the drive of the poem is elsewhere, in the
conversational interchange. But the section recovers in a
marble, final line clinched by the rhyme or half-rhyme;
this has all the strength and sense of powerful, complete
speech that yet admirably fits the measure and takes up
its prepared place with born assurance:

> And thereupon
> That beautiful mild woman for whose sake
> There's many a one shall find out all heartache
> On finding that her voice is sweet and low
> Replied, 'To be born woman is to know—
> Although they do not talk of it at school—
> That we must labour to be beautiful.'

The labour entailed upon the poet, upon the beautiful woman, and upon the learned, toiling lover, works towards the concluding symbol of the poem: the rising moon, dead tired with labouring, emblematical of accomplished beauty that exhausts its vitality in the moment of achievement, and is worn out by time.

The new majesty declares itself beyond all doubts in a group of poems about Maud Gonne in the next collection *The Green Helmet and Other Poems* (1910), beginning with "A Woman Homer Sung" and ending with "Against Unworthy Praise."[5] The basic tongue of these seven poems is the language of a man's conversation with himself, sufficiently shaped and formalised by measure and rhyme to acquire the strength of final statement, as in these lines from "Peace":

> 'Were not all her life but storm,
> Would not painters paint a form
> Of such noble lines,' I said,
> 'Such a delicate high head,
> All that sternness amid charm,
> All that sweetness amid strength?'

The immediate gesture of the speaker is ever present in these "thoughts," and each poem is made living and continuous by the pursuit of the logic in feeling and thought: "why should I blame her for making misery and violence about her? what else could she have done? is she not a second Helen?" ("No Second Troy"); or "I was like the king in the play, prevented from loving by a word; he found happiness at last, but I, who am not a fictive being like him, know what I have lost in life and do not know that I shall recover it in heaven" ("A King and No King"). The Helen-association, chosen for Maud Gonne, emblematises the double vision—each poem a centre where antitheses meet: a ruinous beauty, that exacts blame and praise. Other antitheses are living/ writing ("Words"), the peace of age/the storm of

outh ("Peace"), the shared private dream, the lonely
public reality of scorn ("Against Unworthy Praise").
Perhaps the most beautiful of these poems is the first, "A
Woman Homer Sung," a poem without flaw. It is
marked particularly by the third and fourth rhyming
lines in each stanza, which quicken the pace, and enhance the stress and suspension of the ensuing line:

> And trod so sweetly proud
> As 'twere upon a cloud,
> A woman Homer sung. . . .

Yeats uses the same technique of interweaving that he
had practised in *The Wind Among the Reeds*, but it is here
immensely invigorated by the terse, striding line and by
the repetition not of words or phrases but of whole lines
("*When I was young*," "*A woman Homer sung*") which bind
the poem like a refrain.

The scale and range achieved by these poems is about
as far as Yeats can go, with entire success, in the verse
written up to about 1917. For we must plot as being well
within this range the group of satirical epigrams and
poems dealing with the work of the theatre and other
Irish controversies ("At the Abbey Theatre," and in
Responsibilities "On Those That Hated the Playboy . . ."
and the poems on the Municipal Gallery controversy, "To
A Shade," "To a Wealthy Man . . .," "Paudeen" and
others[6]). The bitterness and masculinity of these poems
remind us of Yeats's old, favourite story about Raftery
cursing the bush that declined to shelter him so that it
withered up. The ancient poet, as Seanchan in *The King's
Threshold* knew, can praise sacred objects but can also
curse the malevolent and the indifferent. The poems
relate to one another by composing a drama in which
different personalities or personifications sustain fixed
antithetical roles. On one side there is the crowd and
its leaders; the speaker's contempt for them is rooted
in comminatory generalisations and purgative dismissals

—"they" ("they are at their old tricks yet"), "Paudeen" and "Biddy," "th'onion-sellers," men who are born to pray and save and fumble in a greasy till ("September, 1913"), the "brazen throat," an "old foul-mouth," eunuchs in Hell; they buy and sell, hunt down the noble quarry, do not understand. On the other side, are their victims, whose labour and service are rejected, all the feeling that is represented by Yeats's attacks in the essays in *Samhain* on newspaper attempts to curb the National Theatre's freedom of expression: "Literature is, to my mind, the great teaching power of the world, the ultimate creator of all values . . . [It] must take the responsibility of its power and keep all its freedom":[7]

One can serve one's country alone out of the abundance of one's own heart, and it is labour enough to be certain one is in the right, without having to be certain that one's thought is expedient also.[8]

The message is Seanchan's, that the poets do not promise safety. The victims are not personifications but Yeats's friends—Hugh Lane, Synge, Lady Gregory—but they are generalised and distanced so as to perform the roles which the poet shapes for them, of men destroyed by popular hatred whose only comfort is the abundance of their own hearts. The third party in the drama is, of course, the poet himself, who performs two interconnected public roles. When addressing those of his own company, as in "To a Friend Whose Work has Come to Nothing" (Lady Gregory), he assumes the urgent but sympathetic voice of the natural teacher and leader: but in "The Fascination of What's Difficult,"—a poem of superb technical assurance—"All Things can Tempt Me," and "A Coat" what is dramatised is his own cursed labour, the share that he has in the victimisation. In so far as these poems are about the alteration in his style, the emergence into conversation, dramatisation,

and forcefulness, the process is described in metaphors of
pain, of shivering, straining, stripping.

   Without abandoning symbol, Yeats admitted into his
verse the dramatisation of personalities and of the poet
as teacher and victim. In *Responsibilities*, too, there
is a group of love-poems, answering to the group in the
earlier volume, of which "Friends"[9] and "The Cold
Heaven" show a deepening of experience and mastery
of line and organisation which make them Yeats's
greatest achievements in this kind. Neither are difficult
poems, although "The Cold Heaven" has at first sight
an irrationality which turns out to be a deep realism: a
linking of experience with inference from it which is
"like life" because it happens so often and is perhaps the
way we perceive the world:

> Suddenly I saw the cold and rook-delighting heaven
> That seemed as though ice burned and was but
>   the more ice,
> And thereupon imagination and heart were driven
> So wild that every casual thought of that and this
> Vanished, and left but memories, that should be
>   out of season
> With the hot blood of youth, of love crossed long
>   ago;
> And I took all the blame out of all sense and reason,
> Until I cried and trembled and rocked to and fro,
> Riddled with light. Ah! when the ghost begins
>   to quicken,
> Confusion of the death-bed over, is it sent
> Out naked on the roads, as the books say, and
>   stricken
> By the injustice of the skies for punishment?[10]

The poet suddenly sees the heaven patterned with burning ice that seems the more icy the more it burns. The
sight overwhelms him, cancelling every contingent thing,
and exposing in its icy glare the central tragic pre-

E

occupation: "the hot blood of youth, of love crossed long ago." In this kind of experience "all the nature murmurs in response if but a single note be touched." The structural link between the burning ice, the burning passion of youth, the coldness against which it strove, develops towards the image in the final lines of the ghost of the dead lover, naked on the roads, punished by the burning from cold skies. "The ghost begins to quicken"— a whole new cycle of expiation for lost love moves into the poem at these words: but 'long ago' has changed into the present and the immediate past, and the language has the urgency, the physical stress ("I cried and trembled and rocked to and fro,/Riddled with light,") of a man speaking out of the centre of a time-span stretching from youth to after-life, in a condition of voice shaken by the wash that a recent experience has left in his mind. It is an experience whose pang is keenest at that *Riddled with light*, the highest point to which the poem mounts in its restless rush of movement and rising rhythms; the punishment began here, the cold heaven agreed and set its sharp instruments to work—in the glare of light which exposed there were the sharp spines which "riddled" like bullets, which made a sieve of the body, or rather—for the strangeness of the punishment suggest this—of the soul, which was already quickening into the ghost, although a moment ago we saw only the body rocking and crying and trembling. For *Riddled with light* is both a high point to which the emotion rises, and also, very vitally, a point of transition; it does not stop the poem, which does not choke with emotion, but leads it on to the franker pictorialisation and bolder rhetoric of the last three lines. As they complete the structure, they also slightly soothe the feeling; this is because they are, relatively, picture and rhetoric, an act of completion as they must be (being the end of the poem), and a slight, necessary withdrawal from the sharp plunge and pain of the middle lines: "the ghost" endures what happens to all ghosts, as the books say; *it* is sent out, in the third person; the poet has withdrawn from his own experience just enough to enable him to finish his artefact.

"The Cold Heaven" is one of Yeats's greatest poems, one of the great lyrics in English, a poem one can never finish describing, and yet which does not need to be described at all, for it describes itself by what it does. Other poems in *Responsibilities*, in their relaxation and gaiety, their conversationalism, and their easy handling of wisdom, give expression to a mood that was to emerge more and more in Yeats's art. There are the five poems about the beggars, the irresponsibles: "The Three Beggars," "The Three Hermits," "Beggar to Beggar Cried," "Running to Paradise," "The Hour Before Dawn."[11] "The Three Hermits," Yeats told Lady Gregory in March 1913, was "my first poem which is comedy or tragi-comedy."[12] Beggars and wanderers, we ought to remember, were not for Yeats simply creatures out of the medieval past, but common enough in the Ireland of his youth. Here he turns them into the *personae* of little moral dramas in order to illustrate his perceptions about human living and the intuitive wisdom of the outcast; they are objectifications, in their way, of the *poète maudit* theme, at once a mockery of his toil ("Running to Paradise"), of his longing for sexual comfort and peace ("Beggar to Beggar Cried"), and a celebration of the artist's freedom from social conventions and middle class ambitions, although we can never be sure whether the third hermit in "The Three Hermits" is a saint or a poet; giddy with his hundredth year, he "sang unnoticed like a bird" while the other two argue about sin and its rewards. In their dramatisation of the outcast, his fears and wisdom, in their humorous speech, and in the curious lightness with which they treat of unaccommodated man, stripped of his lendings when all boughs are bare, they have a Shakespearian quality which looks back to *The Hour Glass* and forward to the

Crazy Jane poems. Their themes link with those of "The Grey Rock,"[13] the longest and most ambitious poem in the volume, about the Rhymers' responsibility to their art, about Florence Farr's longing for an impossible love, and about Cuchulain.

The poem is deeply ambiguous, although Yeats may not have meant it to be. Cuchulain chooses to keep his covenant with the sword, with the hero's life and the death that follows, rather than with Aoife, his immortal mistress, who had promised him two hundred years in the heaven of her love. We see this from Aoife's point of view as a betrayal: Cuchulain should have kept faith with his immortality, as the Rhymers did with their Muse, and the narrator's comments, all but one, enforce this reading. But the lines on Florence Farr suggest the frustration that attends upon such immortal longings, and Cuchulain makes the same kind of choice that he makes later on in *The Only Jealousy of Emer* and *The Death of Cuchulain*, doomed but noble, an assertion of his place in life and of his heroic identity. After all, Yeats himself, like the merry rogue in "The Hour Before Dawn", rejected the immortal lures, and, unlike the men whom he called "the tragic generation" (the Rhymers), lived on and wielded his sword. Was their devotion to the "Muse's sterner laws" really a submission to the longing for death? Was Cuchulain's acceptance of life-and-death the true form that the human tragedy should take? "The Grey Rock" is difficult because its point of view (Aoife's and the narrator's) conflicts with what the story seems to say; but the story itself, Aoife's drama, ends in her being drenched in happy forgetfulness by the wine of the gods —so immortal suffering is easily ended after all, and there is an implicit contrast with human tragic pain: it expects no such end and nobly asserts its allegiance to human living. The poem is important not only because it anticipates themes in the later plays and poems, but because it is an ambitious attempt to link Irish mythology with the dramatisation of men whom Yeats knew and to see them both in a common perspective of tragic and symbolic meaning—the process that was soon to be extended in *A Vision*. But as a long poem it is not perfectly articulated. For that we must turn to the next volumes.

In them Yeats achieves magniloquence, final authority and self-possession. Although development and the discovery of new techniques and interests do not cease, these are most plain in the song-like poems (some forty-seven of them) in the groups sub-titled "A Man Young and Old" (*The Tower*) "Words for Music Perhaps" and "A Woman Young and Old" (*The Winding Stair*). As for the rest of the poems in *The Wild Swans at Coole* (1919), *Michael Robartes and the Dancer* (1921), *The Tower* (1928) and *The Winding Stair* (1933), they constitute Yeats's central achievement; it seems appropriate to select from all four volumes what may best illustrate some characteristics of the achievement as a whole.

The centre of gravity is the "I" created and dramatised by the poet. He now has properties, surrounds himself with emblems and locates himself in a personal landscape having a certain imaginative order. On the map, this country is not so much the Sligo of his youth, Lough Gill, Ben Bulben, and the shore of Rosses, as the countryside south of Galway—Thoor Ballylee, Coole Park, and the stony lands on the borders of Clare. This is the landscape of "In Memory of Major Robert Gregory," "A Prayer for my Daughter," "Meditations in Time of Civil War," and many other major poems. It is a landscape which is granted its own solid identity—it is not ridiculous to go on pilgrimages there, if only to see how closely Yeats's descriptions correspond to the facts—but at the same time we see the poet's mind constantly at work upon it transforming it into emblem. The process turns each poem of this kind into an articulated meditation in which the identity of things is constantly being raised to a new power by the activity of thought, but which is controlled by a reverence both for what the mind makes of things and for what they are. In a poem such as "Coole and Ballylee, 1931" devotion to place is wrought together with the mind, the creator of analogies, into a perfect balance that itself releases a new surge of feeling as it is contemplated by the poet:

> Under my window-ledge the waters race,
> Otters below and moor-hens on the top,
> Run for a mile undimmed in Heaven's face
> Then darkening through 'dark' Raftery's
>   'cellar' drop,
> Run underground, rise in a rocky place
> In Coole demesne, and there to finish up
> Spread to a lake and drop into a hole
> What's water but the generated soul?[14]

This is the subject mentioned in "Dust Hath Closed Helen's Eye" in *The Celtic Twilight* (though the poem that corresponds most to that is the second section of "The Tower"); it was written about by Lady Gregory in her *Coole* (1931):

> Our own river that we catch a glimpse of now and then through hazel and ash ... has ever been an idler. Its transit is as has been said of human life 'from a mystery through a mystery to a mystery'; suddenly appearing, as a French writer has put it, 'dans le beau parc privé de Coole, derrière le village de Kiltartan.' ... Then, flowing free, it helps to form a lake whose fulness, finding no channel above ground is forced 'de chercher sa route par les passages souterains de lac vers la mer'; into which it flows under the very shadow of the Dun of the ancient legendary King Guaire.[15]

Lady Gregory's description, although it shares the impulse to see the landscape as a source of meanings, does not fashion the two together by the unifying power of a style which transmits the mind's intensity. And because it is not articulated her "mystery" lacks the drama of Yeats's sudden question "What's water but the generated soul?"—a thought which Yeats found in the "wise Porphyry."[16] The poem continues to be controlled both by the landscape and by the impulse of mind. First the stormy wood on the lake's borders, the sound of the mounting swan, "Another emblem there!" The meditation on this emblem in the third stanza centres the poem on the speaker so that the transition from the lake to the inside of Coole House in the fourth stanza is not felt to be a break in the order; we are carried along on the poet's senses and feelings ("Sound of a stick upon the floor. . . . Old marble heads, old pictures everywhere . . .") which expand hugely in the last two stanzas into the meditation on "traditional sanctity and loveliness." The crowding of these stanzas with properties and lists ("Great rooms . . . ancestral trees/Or gardens. . . . Marriages, alliances, families") thickens the stream of association so that it seems natural that the poet, at first alone in his meditation by the lake, abruptly introduced into the natural landscape by the question in the first stanza, should now speak for a company ("We were the last romantics . . ."); and the poem ends with a dramatic counter-turn to this in which the loneliness and loss of direction of even this proud company is represented by the riderless horse and the swan drifting upon the darkening flood.[17]

In many of his poems, Yeats was now able to transform his contemporaries and friends into constituent parts of his own drama without losing a sense of their living presence. Such a poem is the companion-piece to the other poem about Coole, "Coole Park, 1929." In its second and third stanzas we can observe the transformation of rooted and sharply characterised men into an emblematic pattern of swallows whirling upon the compass-point of the house and its owner. Other examples are "Upon a Dying Lady" in which the grace and courage and playfulness of the dying Mabel Beardsley are real enough (see Yeats's letters to Lady Gregory in January and February 1913)[18] and yet the whole series constitutes an elegy on the art of living and dying as Yeats now saw it in the perspective of an experience that stretched from the Rhymers to the ritual of tragedy. The Mabel Beardsley series is not massively articulated as is that other elegy, "In Memory of Major Robert Gregory."[19] It is the great example of all those poems by Yeats in which he interprets the character and destiny of his friends and by "getting them in order," like his ideas, transforms them into human images of his convictions. The interpretation, like the working-out of the ideas, is a passionate one; it is a matter of allegiance, love and knowledge, or of a complex, engaged, bitter or tender irony. The elegy on Gregory illustrates the first, as the poems on the Irish revolutionaries illustrate the second.

Yeats had a few months earlier, in March 1918, written another elegy on Lady Gregory's son, who was killed in action in January. The pastoral conventions of "Shepherd and Goatherd" were suggested primarily by Spenser's elegy on Sidney, *Astrophel*; these conventions give an air of pastiche to the whole poem and muffle the ambitious attempt to represent not only the worth of the dead man, but the fortitude of the bereaved mother and the fate of the dead man's soul. The latter is envisaged in the Goatherd's concluding song "He grows younger every second"[20]—fine verses, and a fine statement of Yeats's belief, as described in "The Gates of Pluto" section of *A Vision*, that the soul of a dead man "dreams the events of his life backward through time" in preparation for rebirth or beatitude.[21] But these verses sort ill with the rest of the poem, and the poet's magniloquence is frustrated by the pastoralism of setting and character. Strangely enough Yeats did not borrow from Spenser the stanza of *Astrophel*, but in "In Memory of Major Robert Gregory," completed in June of the same year, he used

for the first time an eight-line stanza borrowed, as has
been shown by Frank Kermode (whose account of the
poem, together with that by Miss Marion Witt, is indis-
pensable),[22] from Cowley's "Ode on the Death of Mr.
William Harvey." "In so doing, he achieves as it were
unconsciously the formal link with the Renaissance hero
that he had unsuccessfully tried for in the pastoral."[23]
For what the poems have in common is the attempt to
represent Gregory as an image of Yeats's convictions
about Unity of Being:

> Somewhere about 1450 . . . men attained to personality
> in great numbers, 'Unity of Being', and became like
> a 'perfectly proportioned human body' . . .[24]

In such subjective men, as Yeats described them, thought
draws its life from the whole body, energy flows outward
from the nature itself; they have become the "joy that is
themselves." But prince and ploughman no longer share
in their dream, the corresponding Unity of Culture
has been shattered long ago, so that the intensity and
isolation required for such an achievement as Gregory's
seemed to Yeats to be something which burns itself up
in the act of accomplishment as "the painter's brush
consumes his dreams".[25] As in the other poem about
Gregory, "An Irish Airman Foresees his Death," the ful-
ness and delight and completed identity of the subjective
man—something which Yeats had tried to represent in
Deirdre and Cuchulain, the joyful energy of a passion
"purified of all but itself"—are seen at the moment
when life finishes in the flare.[26]

The elegy is superbly articulated, and is the best
demonstration of Yeats's new power to organise a poem
greater in length than the interwoven but brief inten-
sities of "The Cold Heaven" or "A Woman Homer
Sung." The setting is the poet's own tower, the landscape of Galway is one which he shares with Gregory;
Johnson, Synge and William Pollexfen, whose imper-

fections are segments of Gregory's circle of perfection, "Our Sidney and our perfect man," are the "lost companions" of Yeats's own dream of literature and ancestry. There is a proud self-involvement that organises all the parts of the poem and sounds in all its stresses and accents; we see the man making the song, drawing us into his place and time, in the formality of a stanza always quickened with feeling—praise whose precise terms for Gregory's accomplishments hold him steadily in the centre of attention, and grief, which is an egotism as well as a tribute, contriving to be both in the superb conceit with which this magniloquent poem ends:

> . . . a thought
> Of that late death took all my heart for speech.

Robert Gregory was represented as an artist who, by the intensity and unity of his life, escaped from self-division and the curse of old age. The poems in which Yeats dramatises the Irish revolutionaries are much more ambiguous in feeling: "Easter, 1916," and the group of which it forms part in *Michael Robartes and the Dancer* (including "On a Political Prisoner"), and "In Memory of Eva Gore-Booth and Con Markewicz" in *The Winding Stair*.[27] Here what Yeats most contemplates is the distortion of the living personality by political hatred. In "Easter, 1916" Yeats sees death as a bewilderment, not as something which completes an image of the human person and leaves it for ever radiant, and he rejects its kindlier synonyms of "sleep" and "night":

> What is it but nightfall?
> No, no, not night but death;
> Was it needless death after all?
> For England may keep faith. . . .[28]

He cannot frame a political hope, and the centre of the poem is the greatly contrived antithesis between the abundant life of the changing stream and the stone, the

stone-like heart of the fanatic, which remains sterile in
its midst. Yet it is the urgent tetrameters of this poem
which give the measure of Yeats's involvement, the
chanting over of the names, and the tone which rocks
from brutal frankness to tender admiration. The poem
achieves no resolution or stay, for the last two lines,
"changed, changed utterly: /A terrible beauty is born"
complete the artefact by bringing it full circle on the
identical lines that ended the first strophe but themselves
reverberate with paradox; the "change" is a violent,
doubtful transformation, achieved once and once only,
unlike the continuous changes and small flowings of the
stream of natural life ("Minute by minute *they* change"),
and the beauty is terrible, drenched in blood. In that
supremely beautiful poem, "In Memory of Eva Gore-
Booth . . ." the tone is more confident, as it is more
tender and gay, mixed with memories of youth: but the
two sisters are similarly images of Yeats's convictions
about the "persecution of the abstract"; the brutality is
the brutality of self-assuredness, as the beauty is the
beauty of tender reverence and regret for an innocence,
a silky ambience, a generous architecture ("Great
windows opening to the south") so vividly realised as to
convey the poet's certainty about where value lies. It is
this certainty, in verse which drops the varying stresses
and numerous half-rhymes of the first part, that transforms the last lines of the poem into an exhortation that
marries courtesy with the daring of the wise fool: "Dear
shadows, now you know it all":

> Arise and bid me strike a match
> And strike another till time catch;
> Should the conflagration climb,
> Run till all the sages know.
> We the great gazebo built,
> They convicted us of guilt;
> Bid me strike a match and blow.[29]

The action does not "make sense" any more than the "great gazebo" can be precisely identified; the merry gesture of nonsensical defiance mocks the whole time-bound, guilt-allotting, comically obsolescent past in which they were all involved. Tom the Lunatic begins to speak here.

Already we sense in these poems the dimunition of personality, the irresponsibility that begins to free itself from the dignity of close-wrought noble speech. But there remains, and always does remain, in Yeats's work a continual return to such magniloquence. In many of the poems, though, Yeats's dialogue is with himself, and is not focussed upon other persons. There are, for example, some ten continuous pages of verse in *The Tower* comprising the fourteen poems grouped as "Meditations in Time of Civil War" and "Nineteen Hundred and Nineteen."[30] Here the speaker presents himself with the greatest degree of circumstantiality, at a cross-roads of time, and in a richly furnished world. Each series moves from the continuously argued metaphorical thought of the first section, the display of the "passionate, reasoning self," through a magnetised chain of personal symbols—tower, sword, birds, dancers, swan and the many clues they provide for the evocation of dramatised patterns of thought and feeling—to end in a bitter and fantastic vision, this time not of actual objects but of evil ghosts, "daemonic images" of hatred and corruption. In its general movement and in its range of voices each series mimes the process which is their common subject, the theme of "The Second Coming", that "Things fall apart; the centre cannot hold." The richness and dignity of the public meditations at the beginning, concerned appropriately enough with rich and famous things, ancestral houses, old gardens, "ingenious lovely things," with how they come to be and with how they are destroyed by the folly of the multitude, by the breakdown amongst the heirs of the tension between the bitterness of the creator and the sweetness of the creation,—these all live on the verge of ruin. As the great structures, magniloquent, abundant with life, permanent and assured, vanish away, and as the voice loses its majestic bitter-sweet strength and sonorous melancholy, there remains the poet in his solitude, half appalled by his implication in all that is gone, yet ready to accept the whirling change of times with stoic fortitude, comforted and yet distracted by the evidence of his own toil, the curious works of his hand and the stately emblems with which he has filled his life; he draws shorter breath; and then mockery or apathy come into the voice—the spectacle is too vile for eloquence:

> A barricade of stone or wood;
> Some fourteen days of civil war;
> Last night they trundled down the road
> That dead young soldier in his blood:
> Come build in the empty house of the stare.[31]

And finally it seems as if the latent frenzy of such thoughts is beginning to loosen the fibres of the speech, to lengthen and disorder the line, and to admit to the mind those evil visions which frightened the narrator in the *Secret Rose* story: "the illusions that creep like maggots into civilisations when they begin to decline, and into minds when they begin to decay."[32] "The Second Coming" has this same pattern and theme much more intensely and tightly drawn.

The structural method employed here comes close to making the poem itself an image of the "conviction." This is perhaps the form that the celebrated last stanzas of "Among School Children" assume. The poem is in part wound upon the same spool of thought as "Adam's Curse" and "Michael Robartes and the Dancer," although it is immensely stronger and richer. The first stanzas make their connexions carefully and logically, in terms of the immediate experience; the sixty year-old smiling public man, which is what the children in the schoolroom see, still bears "your image that blossoms a rose in my heart," and the presence of the children drives him to make comparisons—"Was *she* like this one, or this one, when a child?"—for he has been thinking of a day of unusual sympathy when she spoke of herself as a child. The sudden heart-catching glimpse of an imagined resemblance reminds him of her present image, the Mantegna-like face of the old woman, and this in its turn is counterparted by the youth/age antithesis turned upon himself, once beautiful, now worn out by labour, "a comfortable kind of old scarecrow;" the *comfortable* and the irony closes the movement with a return to the humorous resignation of the first stanza. So far the progress of the poem has represented the natural movement of thought and feeling stimulated by the visit to the schoolroom. In the next two stanzas, the hiding-places of thought open, and two violent movements blow us right away from the schoolroom, the poet, and his visual images of his lady, into the kingdoms of anguish, uncertainty and scorn from whence arise the convictions that "sustain us in defeat or give us victory." In another sense, of course, the subject of these two stanzas relates clearly enough to the theme of childhood and education and its ending in old age after all that labour. But all the meditative repose, the responsiveness to inward and outward things and the "comfortable" irony, has vanished before the tragic urgency of the fifth stanza and the mounting scorn of the sixth: "Plato . . . solider Aristotle . . . world-famous golden-thighed Pythagoras," great men, the issue of the pangs of labour, infinite labourers themselves, are after all just scarecrows. But the child, the two concluding stanzas say, is worshipped as an image by the mother, as the poet worships the image of the lady or the nuns their holy images of bronze and marble:

Both nuns and mothers worship images,
But those the candles light are not as those
That animate a mother's reveries,
But keep a marble or a bronze repose.
And yet they too break hearts—O Presences
That passion, piety or affection knows,
And that all heavenly glory symbolise—
O self-born mockers of men's enterprise;

Labour is blossoming or dancing where
The body is not bruised to pleasure soul,
Nor beauty born out of its own despair,
Nor blear-eyed wisdom out of midnight oil.
O chestnut-tree, great-rooted blossomer,
Are you the leaf, the blossom or the bole?
O body swayed to music, O brightening glance,
How can we know the dancer from the dance?[33]

The invocation in the first stanza quoted is addressed to a
beauty which is often terrible, to the completions of
heaven, to what is symbolised by Fand, the goddess who
is also a witch, in *The Only Jealousy of Emer*, something
beyond human life and yet the final compulsion of the
human imagination. These heavenly images are beyond
the flux of the labouring imagination that has gone to
make them; they symbolise the glory of paradise where
men toil not neither do they spin. They break the heart
because humankind, as Cuchulain shows in the same play,
"cannot stand very much reality," but they are at the
same time the human dream of perfection. Their presence is therefore invoked when the poet comes to his
final statement about what human life itself should
ideally be like—a man not toiling with his life like
children in a school, but a radiant unity of being, like
dancer and blossoming chestnut-tree; never, therefore,
"weary-hearted" like the characters in "Adam's Curse,"
no part of him bruised by labours for the sake of some

other part, but instead answering to that old dream of Owen Aherne in *The Tables of the Law*:

> I know nothing certain as yet but this—I am to become completely alive. . . . I shall create a world where the whole lives of men shall be articulated and simplified as if seventy years were but one moment, or as if they were the leaping of a fish or the opening of a flower.[34]

The final invocations re-state this, as does the fountain, the abounding jet, of the first section of "Meditations in Time of Civil War," which never stoops "to a mechanical/ Or servile shape, at others' beck and call." This is the condition of "uncomposite blessedness" more coolly celebrated in "Michael Robartes and the Dancer." But in this poem, the two invocations in the final stanzas imitate the surge of conviction in a movement that is like that of the abounding jet itself.

"Among School Children" is amongst the most difficult of all Yeats's poems, and in conjoining the vision of heavenly perfection with a vision of the ideal human life, goes a stage further than even the most famous of all, the two Byzantium poems. In these death alone permits an ideal life.[35] Like "Leda and the Swan," the Byzantium poems gain much of their effect from being manifestly based on a rich substratum of ideological and pictorial experience, and have therefore exacted a multiplicity of commentary. To read them in the light of "Among School Children" is to understand them more easily. In "Sailing to Byzantium" the old man moves out of life into the kingdom of the image, where dwell "the self-born mockers of man's enterprise," in the life beyond life. This kingdom is called Byzantium because Yeats, as a celebrated passage in *A Vision* shows,[36] liked to think of early Byzantium as a sacred city where man had attained unity of being and unity of culture. The poet rejects, or is forced by old age to reject, the life of sensual music, of begetting and bearing, a world of procreation, which, because it is so, is also a world that continually dies; unwilling to be an old scarecrow or a dying animal, he seeks to "make his soul" in its final form; the metaphor he chooses for this is a golden bird singing in Byzantium upon its golden branch. This bird is the soul; unlike the birds of the first stanza, it is no longer subject to death; it is a poet's soul that sings to lords and ladies; it is an artefact ("such a form as Grecian goldsmiths make") and therefore "Keeps a marble or a bronze repose," like the artefacts in "Among School Children"; it cannot be betrayed by "honey of generation." "Byzantium" is superficially a more kinetic, but also a more obscure poem. In it Byzantium is seen as a purgatory; on the one side the golden bird, the starlit dome, the purgatorial flame, the smithies where souls are wrought into images, the dancing-floor where they dance out their dance of expiation like the girl in the Noh play; on the other, the "fury and the mire of human veins," the drunken soldiery, the blood-begotten spirits. The poem begins in the historical Byzantium which yet contains in it the antitheses that characterise the visionary one, represented by the "unpurged images of day" stressed against the starlit dome of Santa Sophia, an artefact; in the second stanza the poet achieves the visionary state, unwinding nature and unwinding flesh, with the aid of his communication with an elemental spirit, a Daemon, that is itself stripped of all windings and is the bare, untramelled "thing itself," unaccommodated ghost. In his vision the poet hails the sacred city or its principal symbol, the golden bird, "miracle," the antithesis of nature, and describes the purgatorial process: the arrival of the blood-begotten spirits on the backs of dolphins, carriers of the dead in classical legend and sculpture, and their participation in a rite of purgation that is primarily a dance. This encounter of human and superhuman is described in great excitement and releases a flood of

F

metaphors deeply interconnected in the long history of Yeats's imagination.

"Sailing to Byzantium" is a better poem than its successor, with a more recognisable pulse of feeling; "Byzantium," despite its dynamism and excitements, is more like what Yeats called a "text for exposition", and might without too much injustice be grouped with the other poems which Yeats used for direct expression of the philosophical mythology which was more elaborately synthesised in *A Vision*—"The Double Vision of Michael Robartes," "Ego Dominus Tuus," "The Phases of the Moon."[37] But whether we regard the Byzantium poems as incorporating a neo-Platonic vision of life after death or as celebrating the work of art as opposed to the work of nature, it is true that they both deal with the last things; the Yeatsian aesthetic, like the Yeatsian eschatology, resolves into a final metaphor that reconciles all metaphors:

> I hail the superhuman;
> I call it death-in-life and life-in-death.[38]

In this way the dialogue of self and soul, and of art and life, both reach a conclusion.

But it is a conclusion which works for this poem only, and the dialogues struggle on elsewhere, some distance from the threshold of Byzantium. They are summarised in "The Choice" and in section VII of "Vacillation":

THE SOUL: Seek out reality, leave things that seem.
THE HEART: What, be a singer born and lack a theme?
THE SOUL: Isaiah's coal, what more can man desire?
THE HEART: Struck dumb in the simplicity of fire!
THE SOUL: Look on that fire, salvation walks within.
THE HEART: What theme had Homer but original sin?[39]

This stylisation of the conflict appears again in the first section of "A Dialogue of Self and Soul,"[40] where the pressure and urgency of the "soul" is no more full and

perfect than the resistance of the "self" absorbed in and
withdrawn by its emblem, the Japanese sword in its
silken covering: "the toil of the living is to free themselves
from an endless sequence of objects."[41] Elsewhere,
thought has rendered life intelligible:

> ... I have straightened out
> Ruin, wreck and wrack;
> I toiled long years and at length
> Came to so deep a thought
> I can summon back
> All their wholesome strength.[42]

But images of the ruined friends remain stubbornly in the
affections, unappeased and crippled by time ("The
Results of Thought"). "Responsibility so weighs me
down" ("Vacillation" V), and repentance that keeps the
heart impure is mitigated by flashes of vitality and self-
content that seem no more enduring than the gleams of
sunlight and the glittering stream ("Stream and Sun at
Glendalough"). "Vacillation" IV shows that this charis-
matic joy is brief:

> ... twenty minutes more or less
> It seemed so great my happiness
> That I was blessèd and could bless.

"At certain moments, always unforeseen, I become
happy. . . . I look at the strangers near as if I had known
them all my life, and it seems strange that I cannot speak
to them: everything fills me with affection, I have no
longer any fears or any needs."[43] For artists seek reality
"with the slow toil of our weakness and are smitten from
the boundless and the unforeseen."[44] The greatest statement of this toil and its assuagement comes in the second
part of "A Dialogue of Self and Soul." "Only the dead,"
says the soul, "can be forgiven" (a statement which
conceals no orthodoxy about the manner of their for-
giving), but the self affirms its allegiance to the crime of

death and birth, and is prepared, like the "Irish Airman,"
to suffer all and bring all to mind:

> I am content to follow to its source
> Every event in action or in thought;
> Measure the lot; forgive myself the lot!
> When such as I cast out remorse
> So great a sweetness flows into the breast
> We must laugh and we must sing,
> We are blest by everything,
> Everything we look upon is blest.[45]

The endless labour might end here and the great bond
of responsibilities be cancelled and torn to pieces in this
lonely impulse of delight. But of course it is not.

Any attempt to assess the central achievement of
magniloquence must recognise the unfaltering nature of
the accomplishment. There is perhaps no series of poems
of comparable length in English where failure or slack
and careless passages are so hard to find. The grace that
comes from labour and an intelligence acutely and pro-
fessionally ordered to the matching of its resources with
its needs make the body of this poetry like that of an
excellent athlete or dancer, a never-failing poise and
satisfaction. Despite the importance of symbols in his
work, Yeats did not, like other symbolist writers, break
down the conventions of his speech so that the symbols
flow buoyantly upon a loose stream of free verse or stand
up as eloquent structures in a desert which supplies no
context and neither time nor place nor person. Rooted
in these, he remained rooted in sequence, syntax, and
obedience to the power of the awakened and constructing mind:

> I discovered some twenty years ago that I must seek,
> not as Wordsworth thought, words in common use, but
> a powerful and passionate syntax, and a complete
> coincidence between period and stanza. Because I

need a passionate syntax for passionate subject-matter
I compel myself to accept those traditional metres that
have developed with the language. Ezra Pound,
Turner, Lawrence wrote admirable free verse, I could
not. I would lose myself, become joyless . . .[46]

The golden bird in the Byzantine poems is a rever-
berator of some strength; it may have been the first form
to appear in his imagination when he conceived the poem.
But in the composition it is something to be worked towards, and built into a fabric which obeys the ordinary
laws of grammar and of stanza. The drafts of the
Byzantine poems published by Curtis Bradford[47] show
the first forms as sentences: "I therefore travel towards
Byzantium . . . I fly from things becoming to the thing
become . . . I fly from nature to Byzantium." The
journey is always to be made through language before we
reach the Sphere, Plotinus's ἐκεῖ, the moment where
everything is intelligible in one throb of the artery.
Therefore there is always present in Yeats's most high-
speaking verse the patient artificer, who wishes above all
to complete the artefact, to round it and finish it, as
God rounds the shell's elaborate whorl; his thumb-mark
is seen in the rhetoric, especially in the way every poem
begins as a full statement and ends with a full statement,
the rhythm, stress, rhyme and emphasis giving expression,
whatever is being said by the line, to that small voice
that sighs above the music "It is finished." Similarly,
the range of portraits and self-portraits in the gallery of
his art is stamped with the artificer's mark; the sitters
obey the artist's imperious will and draw their inward
life from his convictions, which range them into order.
But they are not arbitrary, or crippled into an unrecog-
nisable shape, but travelled towards through the language of relationship, allegiance, tenderness and respect,
a language which can be used in the second section of
"The Tower" even for the fictive beings chosen from

Yeats's own stories. So they retain life and seem freely to play their chosen roles in the great mythology.

It is the presence of the artificer that, paradoxically enough, makes it possible to say that, in a sense, Yeats never succeeded in achieving his early ambition of "getting a style." Of course that dense coat of golden mail or those chill notes of the pipe are recognisable as his alone—but there is no style in the sense that there is no Parnassian, to use Hopkins's term, no achieved manner, grand or otherwise, which can be appliquéd to the convictions. We never feel, as we often do with Wordsworth or Milton, that the style has become a habit, and that the poet continues to use it, and even by the ingrained effrontery of his professionalism to achieve a precarious kind of success, when the situation has made that set of gestures inappropriate, too low, or too high. Yeats, the evidence shows, usually composed with enormous difficulty,[48] beginning on each poetic occasion at the beginning, not borrowing his style or solutions from his other poems; he works each time towards the style, not with it; the Byzantium drafts show him turning out several "amateur" poems (of which the most that could be said is that they are extremely promising) as preliminaries to the final version. Perhaps this effort communicates itself in all he does in the magniloquent manner and is responsible for the feeling that each poem has a finality and completeness of utterance that are fresh for every occasion. The poems connect with each other by what can be extrapolated from them by the critic—ideas, symbols, *personae*—rather than as total poems. In this way each poem is an experience that falls back upon itself, like the fountain's abounding glittering jet; each poem is an image of the subjective man; they have become the joy that is themselves.

The poems which have just been discussed are those which Yeats called "poems of civilisation."[49] The poet speaks with his full voice, with much subtlety of thought, and the verse is organised as an expression of a complex

range of experience, which does not achieve any final
resolution except in the completion of the poems themselves. If the artificer is satisfied there, if the soul is strong
with vision or the self able to accept, self-and-soul are
not. The search for wisdom and the spiritual life, the
"intellectual joy of eternity,"[50] falls back again into the
sensual music, from which, indeed, it is never wholly
freed. The search for a society and an audience, although
it can be formulated in "The Fisherman," admits also
that this "wise and simple man" is

> A man who does not exist,
> A man who is but a dream,[51]

It encounters "the daily spite of this unmannerly town,"
is filled with rage because lives are deformed by political
hatred, and dreams frankly of the impossible joys of
ignorance and of detachment from the "old bitter world
where they marry in churches" ("The Dawn," "The
Collar-Bone of a Hare"). This dream is known to be an
inadequate counter-affirmation, the "half-deceit of some
intoxicant," to Yeats's sense of the "growing murderousness of the world,"[52] which is expressed in "The Second
Coming" and in "Nineteen Hundred and Nineteen": he
who can read the signs,

> . . . who knows no work can stand,
> Whether health, wealth or peace of mind were spent
> On master-work of intellect or hand,
> No honour leave its mighty monument,
> Has but one comfort left: all triumph would
> But break upon his ghostly solitude.
>
> But is there any comfort to be found?
> Man is in love and loves what vanishes,
> What more is there to say?[53]

If the ending is not despair, it is because Yeats, in a
sudden upsurge of physical and artistic energy, turned

away from the poems of civilisation and magniloquence
back to the heroic character, to "creative joy separated
from fear," and to a franker sexuality than he had ever
before expressed. The theme of all the poems in "A Man
Young and Old," "A Woman Young and Old" and
"Words for Music Perhaps" is a half-ironic, half-elegiac
justification of sexuality in a naked world which has the
final discipline and stylisation of a very bare playing-
place. It is a huge, sparse world with a few prototypical
characters—the man, the woman, the moralist, Crazy
Jane, Jack, the thorn-tree, ghosts, the constellations. It is
a world where speech grows close to song, and magniloquence has yielded to double-talk, epigram, and refrain.
"I am still of opinion that only two topics can be of the
least interest to a serious and studious mind—sex and the
dead."[54] Repentance no longer keeps the heart impure,
and in "A Man Young and Old" the experience of love
is personal and secret and at the same time transformed
into universal parable. The names of the characters,
Madge, Peg, Peter, here and in the other two series,
symbolise the stripping down to a beggarly wisdom,
which by being bare—an image of essential life freed of
circumstantiality—makes the largest claims for its arche-
typal nature, and talks easily of Paris and Helen, who are
part of this universal skiagraphy of love:

> Though Margery is stricken dumb
> If thrown in Madge's way,
> We three make up a solitude;
> For none alive to-day
> Can know the stories that we know
> Or say the things we say:
>
> How such a man pleased women most
> Of all that are gone,
> How such a pair loved many years
> And such a pair but one,

Stories of the bed of straw
Or the bed of down.[55]

This is the Old Man speaking, but the series begins with
the Young Man, his body transformed to stone by her
lunar kindness ("Human Dignity"); her own heart is
like the lunar stone ("First Love"), and this stone appears
later, cradled in the bosom of the mad and old ("The
Friends of his Youth," "His Wildness"), for this myth
continually points to the analogies between sexual and
maternal love. The rhythms of the poems convey a lilting
tenderness, and this is often coupled with a formally
harsh vocabulary—words such as *lout*, *cosseting*, *a
pushing man*, gestures such as "fell the one in t'other's
arms," "the heart thumps at my side." These, like the
names, make the implicit claim that we are down at the
rock and the source.

In "A Woman Young and Old" an arch of experience
is constructed: from the first innocent coquetry through
flirtatious dissembling, improvisation and game, consum-
mation heavenly and tragic—to unrepentant memory
and quarrel in old age. Its centrepiece is two very great
poems, "Chosen" and "Her Vision in the Wood,"
separated by the aubade "Parting." In "Chosen" the
lover is seen moving or whirling in relation to the woman
like the sun through the figures of the Zodiac round the
body of the earth; after daybreak, he leaves her:

I struggled with the horror of daybreak
I chose it for my lot![56]

For this horror of loss is also the moment of stillness,
when the lovers seem to exchange hearts, and so the
point where the Zodiac is "changed into a sphere," when
the whirling diagram of change, the spiral, is miracu-
lously transformed into the heavenly condition of perfection and rest, where "we may escape from the constraint of our nature and from that of external things,

entering upon a state where all fuel has become flame."[57]
The poem is learned, Elizabethan and metaphysical,
urbane and passionate at the same time. "Her Vision in
the Wood" shows Yeats using a better-known mythology:
the Adonis ritual traces out its calmly passionate
pageant, a stately and immortal artefact, but is transformed into a terrible reality when the woman, now old,
and torn by love-longing, recognises her lover in its
central personage, the dying, castrated huntsman:

> All stately women moving to a song
> With loosened hair or foreheads grief-distraught,
> It seemed a Quattrocento painter's throng,
> A thoughtless image of Mantegna's thought—
> Why should they think that are for ever young?
> Till suddenly in grief's contagion caught,
> I stared upon his blood-bedabbled breast
> And sang my malediction with the rest.

> That thing all blood and mire, that beast-torn wreck,
> Half turned and fixed a glazing eye on mine,
> And, though love's bitter-sweet had all come back,
> Those bodies from a picture or a coin
> Nor saw my body fall nor heard it shriek,
> Nor knew, drunken with singing as with wine,
> That they had brought no fabulous symbol there
> But my heart's victim and its torturer.[58]

The intercourse between symbol and actuality, the way
one is fleshed upon the other, which is so vital in Yeats,
is superbly represented in these two poems: in the one,
love is transformed into an image exempt from time,
deathless with its perfect life, like the Byzantine bird;
in the other an image of this kind is violently converted
into the fury and the mire of human veins. These meeting-places are those where Yeats's most reverberating
poems occur, at the point where Zeus is joined with
Leda, or a magical image slouches to put on flesh

("Leda and the Swan," "The Second Coming"), or
"The Mother of God" asks:

> What is this flesh I purchased with my pains,
> This fallen star my milk sustains?

In speaking of this mystery, they put in a claim for asser-
tive poetry and talkative religion, which are seen, indeed,
as standing or falling together upon what they have in
common.

Many of the poems in "Words for Music Perhaps"
were written in the spring of 1929, on the rebound from
serious illness: "I want them to be all emotion and all
impersonal," he wrote, ". . . I am writing more easily
than I ever wrote and I am happy, whereas I have always
been unhappy when I wrote and worked with great
difficulty."[59] Crazy Jane is a dramatisation of that casting
out of remorse which was celebrated by the Self in "A
Dialogue of Self and Soul" and of the Lunatic's faith in
"Tom the Lunatic":

> Whatever stands in field or flood
> Bird, beast, fish or man,
> Mare or stallion, cock or hen,
> Stands in God's unchanging eye
> In all the vigour of its blood.

So Crazy Jane argues with the Bishop, relying not on
God but on sensual energy and heroic joy. But the sweetness of her triumph in forcing old age to accept all the
natural life of youthful desire, all its conditions and
memories, is conveyed in rhythms that are tempered
and made poignant by the imminence of death; the basic
dramatic situation is that of a lonely, wild, even per-
secuted, old woman, whose lover Jack the Journeyman,
once straight and wild and young, is long since folded
into the pathos of the dead. This situation qualifies the
heroic self-possession of Crazy Jane, her wit and joy;

and elsewhere in the group there is sorrow at the trans-figurations of time ("Girl's Song," "Her Anxiety," "Love's Loneliness," "I am of Ireland")—these poems are elegies which frankly mourn the commonest of lots and of commonplaces, that "Time runs on," that

> Earth in beauty dressed
> Awaits returning spring.
> All true love must die,
> Alter at the best
> Into some lesser thing.
> *Prove that I lie.* [60]

Although Crazy Jane's splendour reflects the creative excitement and energy that Yeats experienced in making the poems, this mournful note sounds behind the urgent conviction of the *persona*, who spits into the face of time, and comes "proud, open-eyed, and laughing"—to the tomb.

As we look back over the long gallery of Yeats's major poems, they have more and more the appearance of some series of Renaissance portraits—say, by Titian, an artist much admired by Yeats, since he, like Raphael and Michelangelo, united intellect and emotion; they have his clarity, and inward authority, and masterful fullness of life, "great hawks at rest."[61] And like traditional paintings they are contained within their frames and shaped to individual finality by composition; they separate from one another in order to assert the more vigorously the life that is in each. It is doubtful, therefore, whether they compose an *oeuvre* in the approved literary sense. It is dangerous to mistake their thematic correspondences and linking symbols for a unity which is lacking: for that is to confuse the ideology and the biography with the works of art which are born from them. There is a sense in which the completest collection of Yeats's poems is still an anthology. After *The Wanderings of Oisin*, Yeats never wrote another "long poem," and it is no use pretending that what we have constitutes one. Perhaps this means that he is not amongst the greatest writers, who usually make larger claims than the painters, and whose old dream is still the epic, the magnificent serial that keeps the tribe awake until dawn. This individuation of the poems may reflect all unwillingly his youthful conviction that the world had become a "bundle of fragments." The nearest, indeed, he comes to the long work is in the plays, especially the Cuchulain series, and to those we must now again turn.

REFERENCES

1. *C. Plays*, p. 196.
2. *E. & I.*, pp. 271–2.
3. *A.*, p. 492.
4. *C.P.*, p. 89.
5. *C.P.*, pp. 100–104.
6. *C.P.*, pp. 119 ff.
7. *E.*, p. 117.
8. *E.*, p. 123.
9. *C.P.*, p. 139.
10. *C.P.*, p. 140.
11. *C.P.*, pp. 124–134.
12. *L.*, p. 577.
13. *C.P.*, pp. 115–119.
14. *C.P.*, p. 275.
15. Lady Gregory, *Coole* (Cuala Press, 1931), pp. 27–8.
16. *M.*, p. 80; cf. *V.* (1937), p. 220.
17. *C.P.*, p. 276.
18. *L.*, pp. 574–575.
19. *C.P.*, pp. 148–152.
20. *C.P.*, pp. 162–163.
21. *V.* (1925), p. 225.
22. Kermode, *Romantic Image* (1957); M. Witt, "The Making of an Elegy," *Modern Philology*, XLVIII (1950), 112–21.
23. Kermode, *op. cit.*, p. 40.
24. *A.*, p. 291.
25. *C. Plays*, p. 594.
26. *C.P.*, p. 151.
27. *C.P.*, pp. 202–207, p. 263.
28. *C.P.*, p. 204.
29. *C.P.*, p. 264.
30. *C.P.*, pp. 225–237.
31. *C.P.*, p. 230.
32. *M.*, p. 276.
33. *C.P.*, pp. 244–245.
34. *C.W.*, VII. 155.
35. *C.P.*, p. 217, 280.
36. *V.* (1937), pp. 279–80.
37. *C.P.*, pp. 192, 180, 183.
38. *C.P.*, p. 280.
39. *C.P.*, p. 285.
40. *C.P.*, pp. 265–66.
41. *M.*, p. 353.
42. *C.P.*, p. 287.
43. *M.*, pp. 364–65.
44. *M.*, p. 340.
45. *C.P.*, p. 267.
46. *E. & I.*, pp. 521–2.
47. Bradford, "Yeats's Byzantium Poems: A Study of their Development," *P.M.L.A.*, LXXV (1960), 110–125.
48. See, for example, *A.*, p. 202.

49. *L.P.*, p. 148.
50. Yeats in a broadcast talk, July, 1937, quoted by Bradford, *op. cit.*, p. 111.
51. *C.P.*, p. 167.
52. *A.*, p. 192.
53. *C.P.*, p. 234.
54. *L.*, p. 730.
55. *C.P.*, p. 254.
56. *C.P.*, p. 311.

57. Unpublished MS, quoted by Ellmann, *The Identity of Yeats* (London, 1954), p. 221; see also Yeats's notes on the poem, gathered in the Variorum edition, pp. 830, 831.
58. *C.P.*, p. 313.
59. *L.*, pp. 758, 761.
60. *C.P.*, p. 297.
61. *A.*, p. 292.

CHAPTER VI

THE PLAYS: SECOND PERIOD
1915–38

Now his wars on God begin;
At stroke of midnight God shall win.
"The Four Ages of Man."

The second period of Yeats's work for the theatre was
preceded by his discovery of the Japanese Noh drama
and entailed his repudiation of a good deal that had been
built up by the Abbey. But the new practice and principles were designed to gratify needs which had made
themselves felt for a long time and which the earlier
Abbey plays had failed to satisfy: "we did not set out to
create this sort of theatre, and its success has been to me
a discouragement and a defeat," he wrote in 1919.[1]

Yeats first heard about the Noh drama from Ezra
Pound in the winter of 1913–14. It gave him the form
and apparatus (a chorus detached from the action,
masked players, a climactic dance, a bare stage with only
a patterned screen) for Four Plays for Dancers: At the
Hawk's Well, 1915–16, The Only Jealousy of Emer, 1916,
The Dreaming of the Bones, 1917, and Calvary, c. 1920—the
dates are those of composition. It influenced a number of
his other plays. Yeats was attracted by the way in which
adaptation of the Noh appeared to free him from all
obligations to the naturalistic stage and to "the
stupidity of an ordinary audience"[2] trained in its conventions. The Abbey, it now seemed to him, had achieved
only the most precarious kind of freedom from an art

founded upon observation and "sympathy,"—the actors copying behaviour that they saw in life, the audience recognising the life of their kind, though in heightened and selected form, on the stage. But Yeats wanted, as he had always wanted, the ritual of passion, "lonely dreaming," a *subjective* not an *objective* theatre, one that was liberated from the conversation of the time and might mediate unity of being, not the "unity of things in the world." Synge and Lady Gregory, "caught between the pull/Of the dark moon and the full" had blurred their individual way of seeing and their elaboration of a personal style with the objective qualities of humour, observation and "a speech founded upon that of real life":

When you [Lady Gregory] and Synge find such an uneasy footing, what shall I do there who have never observed anything, or listened with an attentive ear, but value all I have seen or heard because of the emotions that they call up or because of something they remind me of that exists, as I believe, beyond the world ?[3]

The solution for the Abbey was to grow ever more objective, "making articulate . . . all the dumb classes of the world, each with its own knowledge of the world, its own dignity, but all objective with the objectivity of the office and the workshop." Its task was to understand and to see, not to feel and to imagine: "Let those who are all personality, who can only feel and imagine, leave it. . . ."[4]

Yeats, as was his way, made his repudiation more dramatic and complete than it really was (most of his later plays still had their first showings on the Abbey stage). But in his seeking to create "an unpopular theatre and an audience like a secret society," he found the Noh wonderfully apposite. He had always been mistrustful of the *painted* stage, the swags and furbelows of the scene-painter, which distracted from the tragic reverie—hence his enthusiasm for the discretion and austerity of Gordon Craig, although collaboration with him had not got much further than the designs which illustrate *Plays for an Irish Theatre* (1911) and the screens for *The Hour-Glass*. The Noh dispensed with all that, just as it achieved the proper subordination of the music to the words: the voice was freed from competition with an orchestra, and accompanied only by drum, flute or zither. Its audience excluded the common people, and evoked the capacity of leisured and lettered persons to grasp allusions and remember traditions and even to be self-consciously proud of their own skill in doing so—to be aware of what Eliot, in another context, called the "simultaneous order and . . . simultaneous existence" composed by the work of dead poets and dead artists:[5] "A poetical passage cannot be understood without a rich memory." Nor does the Noh player learn his art by the observation of life but by going within, to his heart and to the common memory, the *anima mundi*.[6] It was pleasing to Yeats to realise that the simplified stage of the Noh did not exclude a sense of sacred and much-legended place, for here was the quality that distinguished his own art, however tentatively practised, in *The King's Threshold*; and he detected also in the Noh plays "a playing upon a single metaphor" (the symbolism of the woven grass in *Nishikigi* is one of his examples) of the kind that he had himself practised, although then quite ignorant of the Noh, in the bird-symbolism of *The Shadowy Waters*, the stars and moon of *The King's Threshold*, or the cage-bird, eagle, hunting and animal metaphors of *Deirdre*. In all this, the Noh seemed to show how instinctively right he had always been.

The discovery of the Noh is linked also with the poetry and philosophical mythology of its period, especially through its climactic dance and its use of masks. In the essay on "The Tragic Theatre" (1910), Yeats had written of the choice of "that beauty which seems unearthly because the individual woman is lost amid the labyrinth of its lines as though life were trembling into stillness and

G

silence, or at last folding itself away." In all tragic art, he thought, in its supreme moments, characterisation and realism are rejected, or only used for purposes of contrast (a favourite example was the old man with the asp in Cleopatra's death-scene): into the places they have left empty, are summoned "rhythm, balance, pattern, images that remind us of vast passions, the vagueness of past times, all the chimeras that haunt the edge of trance."[7] This was the effect that, by merely verbal means, Yeats had sought after, and failed to achieve, in Deirdre's tragic reverie and Seanchan's lifting-up. Character, näively human, the definition of individuality, would keep breaking in and frustrating that breaking down of the dykes which separate man from man. In the Noh dance Yeats discovered a means of overcoming these frustrations; the dance is "a series of positions and movements"; for the Japanese dancers,

> the interest is not in the human form but in the rhythm to which it moves, and the triumph of their art is to express the rhythm in its intensity. . . .

The face, like the faces of all the actors, is masked, "nor shall we lose by stilling the movement of the features, for deep feeling is expressed by a movement of the whole body."[8] The painted real face, expressing some commonplace player's vulgar notion of vitality, is banished along with the painted scene; the immobility and austerity of the mask substitute for flesh an artefact, a dead face which is the more alive, like the golden bird of Byzantium, because it is unchanging and because it is liberated from time and the sensual music; it is "plummet-measured," like the statues of Phidias:

> His numbers, though they moved or seemed to move
> In marble or in bronze, lacked character.[9]

It was this lack that "made the people stare," but those who are initiated by passion, those who "are accustomed

to faces of bronze and of marble," understand that the
ritual of passion and the intensity of being are most unin-
terruptedly expressed by keeping "an appropriate
distance from life."[10] "It is even possible," Yeats wrote,
"that being is only possessed completely by the dead, and
that it is some knowledge of this that makes us gaze with
so much emotion upon the face of the Sphinx or of
Buddha."[11] The masked dancer is an "image of those pro-
found emotions that exist only in solitude and in
silence,"[12] purified of all except themselves.[13] The movements of his dance transcend words and character. The
dancer became for Yeats the symbol that most perfectly
expressed, as in the last stanza of "Among School
Children," that "completely alive" condition of unity of
being, where no aspect of life is sacrificed to some other
part, where the body is not bruised to pleasure soul, nor
does the poet labour in dark misery to engender beauty;
and this is because in the dance we cannot distinguish
between what it is and what it means; its movements,
its "body," *are* what it means, its "soul;" and it therefore
emblematises also the symbolist ideal of what a poem
should be, something in which all intellectual effort is
assimilated into the poem's body, meaning and form are
identical, its body thinks. The strength of this conviction
and this ideal[14] support the primacy which Yeats now
gives to the dance in his plays.

In these plays, then, verse, ritual, music and dance, in
association with action, were to be wrought into a unity
with gesture, costume, and facial expression to make of
each play a self-subsistent image that would "recede
from us into a more powerful life," the deep of the mind,
the *anima mundi*.[15] By these means the door will be shut
against abstraction, against separable intellectual content, against that "something impersonal"—"Society,
fate, 'tendency' "—which, Yeats had complained, come
into the story when the dramatist ordinarily sets out to
construct plots and arrange characters.[16] Measured

against an ideal unity of this kind, the unity of the symbolist poem, the pieces in *Four Plays for Dancers* do not succeed. Rejoicing in his new freedom from the ordinary audience, Yeats filled the plays with the convictions that he was systematising in *Per Amica Silentia Lunae* and *A Vision* and derived from a lifetime of meditation on "unknown thought." F. A. C. Wilson, who has explained these sources so well in his two books, is right to refer to them as the "metaphysical implication behind the verse,"[17] and all the plays appear to contain unresolved residues of meaning, especially in the Musicians' songs, which injure their self-possession. Furthermore, the heroic character is hard to assimilate to the unity of the Noh image. The presence of this character was inevitable as soon as Yeats decided—and he could never have avoided such a decision, for it was a major determinant of his interest in the form—to present Irish mythology in the Noh guise. "It pleases me," he wrote at the end of the Introduction to Pound's *Certain Noble Plays of Japan*,

> to think that I am working for my own country. Per-haps some day a play in the form I am adapting for European purposes may excite once more, whether in Gaelic or in English, under the slope of Slieve-na-mon or Croagh Patrick, ancient memories. . .[18]

When the holy mountains of Ireland rise up, when Cuchulain appears, we may wonder about Lady Cunard's drawing-room, and those leisured and lettered people for whom Yeats designed his unifying image. Contradictions of the kind implied here run through all the plays and make them, in a general judgment, more human and less remote and aristocratic than the theory demanded.

For what the four plays depict, though the details of their stories differ a great deal, is not so much the image out of time and deathless as the struggle against it. The dialogue of Self and Soul breaks out again, and Cuchulain

especially, trailing with him the old frustrations and
tragic ironies of *On Baile's Strand*, mediates afresh the
declaration of the self, the unfinished man and his pain
and the finished man among his enemies.[19] These plays,
have their existence at the point where being delivered
from the crime of death and birth into the quarter where
all thought is done descends upon the self as something
that robs it of identity and even presents a face of magnificent evil, that of the demon and not of the Daimon. This
is not, perhaps, what the plays say, but it is what they
act out. It has to be observed, for example, that the
climactic dance in *At the Hawk's Well*, whatever its place
in an initiatory rite which Cuchulain fails to accom-
plish, is an evil vision which lures him away from the
unity of being symbolised by the plashing water in the
well and, dominating the play, effectively substitutes itself for the much less effectual symbol of the well, which
ought to be the true object not only of the hero's concern
but of the theatrical strategy. But the well is displaced in
more than one sense. The Guardian of the well is far
more important than the well itself, and seems in the
context of the hero's quest, to say something about the
unifying image which the well's pleasant and traditional
symbolism conceals. "O God protect me," says the First
Musician,

> From a horrible deathless body
> Sliding through the veins of a sudden.[20]

Cuchulain, the subjective hero, here encounters the
dancer as witch, hawk, destroyer of his subjectivity with
its own, for the subjective seeks always to transform
others into his objects. Cuchulain's inborn courage which
enables him, unlike his foil the Old Man, to gaze into
the hawk's eyes, also earns him the hawk's curse of self-
division, snatching him from unity and determining the
murderous, broken pattern of his days:

Never to win a woman's love and keep it;
Or always to mix hatred in the love;
Or it may be that she will kill your children . . . [12]

The Noh dance, if it is to be identified as the point where
"labour is blossoming," has here suffered a transformation by being put into the context of a heroic life, the
obstinate identity and heroic criminality of the self that
asserts its "soldier's right" to the adventure which, in
promising salvation, gives destruction. At the end of the
play Cuchulain is left with only his name:

He comes! Cuchulain, son of Sualtim, comes![22]

But this assertion of identity assures his place amongst
the tragic heroes, "things emblematical of love and war,"
in the kingdom of the self and the sensual music, not of
the dead, smiling face of Sphinx or Buddha. The hero
who seeks the unifying image—and for that reason is
nobler than the chorus who praise a "pleasant life/
Among indolent meadows" or the Old Man who fears
pain—encounters in this play a terrible manifestation of
it; for such presences break hearts. A similar imagining
controls *Calvary*. It is a play which makes use of Yeats's
conception of the Christian era as a civilisation antithetical to that of Greece and Rome, which, grown calm
and abstract, now begins to shudder and cry out as a
violent reversal of all its ways approaches; and it uses too
the notion of "dreaming-back," the re-living of the events
of life by the dead, which Yeats was working out in *A
Vision* and had written about in "Shepherd and Goatherd." But formally and theatrically its structure expresses the struggle of subjective men against the god who
invades the soul. In the centre of the stage is Christ, in
his "dreaming-back," a rigid Pantocrator, a Byzantine
image, which demands a total allegiance; the other
persons in the play, Lazarus, Judas, and the Roman
Soldiers, strive to preserve their loneliness and self-
possession against this surrender to a god who wishes to

change everything into himself. Nobody "wins" in this play, which holds the conflicting elements stiffly inter-locked, the masked Christ against the dance of the Soldiers, "Three old gamblers who have asked for no-thing"; their self-delight is in its turn contrasted with the despair of Lazarus and Judas, whose selfhood, even their personal death, is threatened by the persecution of Christ.

The Only Jealousy of Emer is the most elaborate of the four plays for dancers. There is no doubt that in his manipulation of Bricriu, the evil spirit who has taken Cuchulain's body, and of the Ghost of Cuchulain, Yeats was interested in finding out "what dramatic effect one could get out of a mask, changed while the player re-mains upon the stage to suggest a change of personality."[23] Also the play is Yeats's most ample attempt at marrying the Noh devices with Irish mythology—the tale of how Cuchulain, after fighting the sea in his madness, is watched over by Emer his wife and his mistress Eithne Inguba. But everything in the play, of which there are several versions, bears upon the central incident; in this it is not difficult to detect a pattern like that of *Calvary* and *At the Hawk's Well*. The supernatural Presence is the Woman of the Sidhe, the dancer, who offers the Ghost of Cuchulain "nothing but the beauty" of a changeless image of love beyond time. A simulacrum of the phase of the Fifteenth Night, the phase of perfect beauty in Yeats's scheme of the correspondences between character and the lunar phases,[24] this dancer tempts in the guise of a ritual test of the hero's capacity to bear this blinding promise—or tests in the guise of a temptation:

> GHOST OF CUCHULAIN: Who is it stands before me there
>   Shedding such light from limb and hair
>   As when the moon, complete at last
>   With every labouring crescent past,
>   And lonely with extreme delight,
>   Flings out upon the fifteenth night?

WOMAN OF THE SIDHE: Because I long I am not
        complete.
    What pulled your hands about your feet,
    Pulled down your head upon your knees,
    And hid your face?
GHOST OF CUCHULAIN: Old memories:
    A woman in her happy youth
    Before her man had broken troth,
    Dead men and women. Memories
    Have pulled my head upon my knees.[25]

The ghost is knotted in the impurity of life, and fails the
test: but we cannot, in the context, read the dancer as
other than an image deeply hostile to human love, which
is here defined—and the definition is also an acceptance
like the joyful acceptance of the Self in "A Dialogue
of Self and Soul"[26]—as incomplete, compromised, "the
wind-blown dirt of memories" according to the Woman
of the Sidhe, but in this play caught up with the heroic
self-sacrifice of Emer, the human nobility of those who
are content with the unfinished man and his pain. Emer,
who, according to the conditions determined by the evil
Bricriu, must renounce Cuchulain's love if he is to
return to life, achieves this renunciation at the last
moment, and restores him to Eithne Inguba's arms from
the immortal embrace. Her sacrifice must renounce the
lover for whose sake it is done—a sufficient comment on
the imperfections which determine human ways of
loving, but at the same time an acknowledgment of their
precarious but decisive authority over a love which cannot die, which cannot lay down its life, which shares the
nature of the artefact. The sexual image desired by the
hero, who is a man of the twelfth Phase, says Yeats, is
"drawn as with a diamond, and tinted those pale colours
sculptors sometimes put upon a statue."[27] The Woman
of the Sidhe is Cuchulain's "statue"; the Musicians lament
the tragedy of the goddess, the "bitter reward," which

the many incarnations that culminated in her perfection have earned ("O bitter reward/Of many a tragic tomb!"), for

> He that has loved the best
> May turn from a statue
> His too human breast.[28]

Bricriu's evil scheme led to this. But the whole play says more, affirming, in the nobility of Emer's gesture—the theatrically central moment of the play in both the final version and in the prose version entitled *Fighting the Waves*—and in the tenderness of the Ghost of Cuchulain's memories, the stubborn actuality of the "too human," which has its own kind of beauty.

Yeats is still dwelling on the theme of *The Shadowy Waters*, the "miraculeuse nuit nuptiale," but has now wrought it into dramatic dialogue which, by specifically theatrical means (Emer's cry of renunciation, the dance, the changing of the masks), interlocks heavenly perfection with human circumstance.

Most of the remaining plays can be divided into those whose vital centre is the masked dancer or a presentation which corresponds to him, and those in which a manifestation of that kind, although always present, is travelled towards through the fortunes of a hero. The first group, which includes *The King of the Great Clock Tower*, *A Full Moon in March*, *The Resurrection*, and *The Words upon the Window-pane* comprises plays in which this manifestation unifies the form more and more, becomes coincident with the play itself, *is* the play, or all that part of it which is not merely preparation and setting of the scene. In the second group—*The Herne's Egg*, *Purgatory*, *The Death of Cuchulain*—the stress is laid upon the hero's struggle, and the resolution of his fate by god or image is kept in the position traditionally accorded to catastrophe, at the end. All these plays have some affinities with the Noh, but they are more obvious in those belonging to the first group. With the second group, it is much easier to talk about characterisation of heroes who continually act out their identities and seek to preserve them, living men who are blind but are content to bear it all again: "Cuchulain, son of Sualtim, comes!"

The Resurrection (1925–30) and The Words upon the Window-pane (1930), both in prose, use their naturalistic scene and dialogue merely as containers to hold reality's flaming torch, and when this torch flares up, the contingencies perish, leaving only the blaze upon the sight. In The Resurrection we return to the themes of Calvary. The Hebrew and the Greek, the one a "subjective" man like Judas, the other the representative of the dying classical civilisation, the builder of order and of cities, argue about their condition as they guard the Apostles of Jesus during the interval between crucifixion and resurrection. As they talk, the streets are loud with the cries of the worshippers of Dionysus who have returned from burying their god, and await his lifting-up; these sectaries, who seem so foul a symptom of disorder to the followers of Jesus, represent the loss of control, the "peacock's cry," of the old primary civilisation as it is about to be transformed into the Christian era.[29] The Greek's theory that Jesus was a spirit who only seemed to bear a human body, the Hebrew's that he was a virtuous man who suffered from the illusion that he was the Messiah, are confirmations of their respective faiths in the old order, and in subjectivity, their freedom from the pantocrator who takes men by their souls and drives them into the desert where the anchorite becomes only an object of the immanent god. The lines of the drama converge steadily upon the moment, preluded by the return of the Syrian messenger with the news that the tomb of Jesus is empty, when the masked Figure of Christ enters the room, and the Greek touches the wounded side of his Idea to find there a beating heart:

O Athens, Alexandria, Rome, something has come to
destroy you. The heart of a phantom is beating. Man
has begun to die.[30]

This moment is the "dance," the point in the play which
most clearly indicates its structural affinity with the
climactic moments of revelation and spiritual enlighten-
ment found in the Noh.[31] And this moment in *The
Resurrection* is perhaps the most brilliantly theatrical to be
found in any of Yeats's plays. Behind it lies the whole
weight of some of Yeats's most compelling poems—
"The Second Coming," "Leda and the Swan," "Her
Vision in the Wood"—and of the meeting-places where
they live, where the god achieves a human body.[32] *The
Resurrection* is not, of course, a Noh play, nor is *The Words
upon the Window-pane*, which describes a séance in a
Dublin lodging-house and the varying commonplace
expectations and curiosities of those who attend it. What
blazes forth in this play is the central image of the suffering Swift, "dreaming back" in his mad old age—a
sustained, painful monologue through the mouth of an
ignorant medium, a contrivance of perhaps even more
theatrical daring than the Figure of Christ in *The
Resurrection* because of its length and the demands it
makes upon the actress. Although these plays have such
contrasting subject-matters, they are very similar in form,
and are really quite unexpected achievements in the
brilliant success with which Yeats turns the tables on the
naturalistic drama (which he had always hated) by, as
it were, exploding it from inside. From its smoking ruins
arises the terrible image of an utterly different kind of
life.

But in the other plays of this group the victory over
naturalism goes by default. *The King of the Great Clock
Tower* (1933–4) and *A Full Moon in March* (1934) are two
versions—the second much more stripped and pruned
than the first—of the same theme, and in both the Queen

is the most absolute of Yeats's dancers. A common man, Stroller, Fool, or Swineherd, swears or prophesies that the Queen will dance for him, that he will sing for her, and that a kiss will emblematise their union. With furious cruelty, the Swineherd is beheaded, and the Queen dances, holding the severed head, which sings. The Musicians' songs celebrate this "miraculeuse nuit nuptiale" and meditate upon the conjunction, in the kingdom where the dance prevails, of austere, royal perfection and the foulness of the unfinished man. This is how the cursed poet is united with the image, which costs him his life but leaves him his song, or how spirit fallen into the material world rejoins the principle from which it emanates.[33] The characters here are swallowed up in their meanings, the form of the drama is almost entirely coincident with the manifestation of the reality, and the *straining* of the being against it has disappeared; such human motives as there are disturb rather than enhance the impersonal authority with which the characters perform their roles: "the interest is not in the human form but in the rhythm to which it moves," but in these plays the rhythm, which is the rhythm of the play itself, is, more exactly than ever before, one which is imposed by the logic of the philosophical mythology and does not flow from the life of the individual character.

It is this life, however, which controls the rhythms of the plays in the second group, *The Herne's Egg* (1935), *The Death of Cuchulain* (1938), and *Purgatory* (1938). All three of them have complicated and subtle stories, and nuances of meaning which depend upon "the metaphysical implication behind the verse." It is this metaphysical implication, the powers that brood within his world and control his fate, which the hero fails to understand; he is not an initiate, as the Swineherd is, into the full complexity of the Yeatsian systems, and in the end he is defeated, like any other fool. Yet the audience is invited to participate at the point where the fallen or incomplete nature of the hero and the net of supernature are held in perspective, the "emotions of a soul dwelling in the presence of certain ideas."[34] The stress is laid upon these emotions and upon the man's sense of what he is, and his ultimate transformation into an animal or a ghost is not of the kind which "proves" anything that can possibly devalue what the play has shown forth about the "accent of *heroic* truth," its courage, ignorance, and self-dependence. Thus in the Ovidian fable of *The Herne's Egg*, Congal, King of Connacht and of Tara, in his ignorance steals the sacred eggs of the bird-god, the Great Herne, and is punished by a fall from the Valhalla of his prelapsarian condition into a world of real war and real death; he decides to take revenge upon the god by violating his priestess Attracta—an act of double consequence, like everything else in this play, for the god uses Congal as his surrogate for his mystic marriage with Attracta and at the same time punishes him for this further sacrilege by ordaining that he shall die meanly at the hands of the Fool. Congal, in a last act of heroic self-possession, resolves to escape this and to defeat the god by taking his own life. He has, in divine fact, died at the hands of a fool. But in his death he asserts the *heroic* fact, the truth that *he* knows:

CONGAL: [*almost screaming in his excitement*] Fool!
    Am I myself a Fool?
  For if I am a Fool, he wins the bout.
FOOL: You are King of Connacht. If you were a Fool
    They would have chased you with their dogs.
CONGAL: I am King Congal of Connacht and of Tara,
    That wise, victorious, voluble, unlucky,
    Blasphemous, famous, infamous man.[35]

From the god's point of view, all that Congal has suffered in the play constitutes a rigid sequence of offence and punishment; but from the hero's point of view, it makes the kind of sense he, in his foolishness, understands to say that he can "fight" and has "beaten" the god. I think that the audience is expected to hold these conflicting testimonies in an equilibrium throughout the play. It seems, therefore, a pity that Yeats makes the balance tilt so decisively towards the god by pursuing Congal after death into his punishment of rebirth as a donkey (Attracta's part in this episode is mysteriously muddled and arbitrary, too). This reduces something hitherto rather Shakespearian to a morality-play, and aligns the dramatist with the philosophical mythologist, anxious to prove that he is right: "The poem may use beliefs but must never seem to have been written merely to express them."[36]

The Herne's Egg is not a Noh play, but *The Death of Cuchulain* more obviously proceeds to the consummating dance. The play itself is a dance of death arranged by the goddess of war. But Cuchulain does not perceive this and asserts his ignorant right to interpret the trap in which he is caught in terms of the life he understands, to fight the battle when he will, and to misread the divine malevolence as Eithne Inguba's merely human and natural jealousy: "I make the truth!" he cries.[37] In the second part of the play, when he is wounded to death and confronts Aoife, it seems that his life has come full circle— the play deliberately retraces in wavering memory and weakening rhythms the patterns of *On Baile's Strand* and *At the Hawk's Well*—and the dying Cuchulain, self-killed by six soldiers in the assertion of his heroic truth, dies again at the hands of a Fool. This double-natured event is heavy with the ironies that attend all Yeats's readings of Cuchulain; Aoife the Revenger, whose act of revenge might have meaningfully completed the story of the death of her son Conlaoch at Cuchulain's hands, is casually supplanted by the Fool; Cuchulain himself, the great fighting-man, has a vision of his soul after death, "a soft feathery shape." But this transformation is much more delicately handled than it is in *The Herne's Egg*. Cuchulain is not punished for what his life has been, but himself acknowledges the irony of his fate and keeps control of it—a wiser fool than Congal; and this tragic wisdom is a completion and a self-achieved reward, an acknowledgment of his full nature and setting as the ironically frustrated hero.

Purgatory was written at the end of the same year (1938), and is Yeats's last play. In its theme it recalls *The Dreaming of the Bones* and *The Words upon the Window-pane*, but whereas in those plays there is dominance by the ghosts, who speak and dance and blaze forth, in *Purgatory* the apparitions are silent and pose in their lighted window while the Old Man, the central character, takes everything upon himself. The scene is a leafless tree and ruined house, before which stand a wandering pedlar and his son. In this house, the pedlar had been born, the son of a great lady who had married a drunken groom. The consequences of this marriage were utterly ruinous: the destruction of the house and the murder of the groom by his son. It is the anniversary of the mother's wedding-night and her shade, "dreaming back" in purgatory, must act the occasion through again and again, tortured by remorse and at the same time renewing her pleasure in her own degradation. The mother, therefore, cannot free herself from this condition, from her "thought" which dwells upon the consequences which her sin has brought to bear upon others—her son degenerate from the noble stock, his son still further degenerate, and so on to generations unborn. In an effort to end this chain of consequence, the Old Man murders the boy. The apparitions vanish, the bare tree puts on leaf, but a moment later the bridegroom's hoofbeats are heard again, and the Old Man realises in despair that the murder of his own son cannot assuage the pain and degradation of his mother's ghost any more than could the murder of his father:

> Her mind cannot hold up that dream.
> Twice a murderer and all for nothing,
> And she must animate that dead night
> Not once but many times!
>
> O God,
> Release my mother's soul from its dream!
> Mankind can do no more. Appease
> The misery of the living and the remorse of
> the dead.[38]

Like the other Yeatsian heroes, the Old Man is defeated by the rigid logic of the supernatural system. But the play is more than a parable about this. It is a study of his mixed nature, his ignorance and his truth, his criminality and his instinct to redress it. He is, like Harry in *The Family Reunion*, "the consciousness of [his] unhappy family," and proceeds—unless this is to attach too much weight to the final lines—to seek God in an attempt to escape from the cruelty of the image. This is as far as any Yeatsian hero gets in his "blind struggle in the network of the stars."[39] It is especially upon that blind struggle in the person of a protagonist, an individual defined and discriminated, that the dramatic weight of *Purgatory* rests. This is a sharp contrast with that impersonality, that withdrawal of character, those faces of bronze and marble, the individual lost amidst the labyrinth of its lines, of which Yeats had written so much.

The Noh imitations were, Yeats wrote, "something that need absorb no-one's life."[40] Throughout the period he experimented a good deal with forms and versifications. In the *Four Plays for Dancers* the blank verse, not greatly different from the verse of *Deirdre*, is already being invaded by the Musician's songs and by the use of a line with four stresses for such intense dialogue as that between the Ghost of Cuchulain and the Woman of the Sidhe. It seems clear that in many of the plays the songs, cryptic, and powerfully stylised, are a kind of psalmody that implicitly claims, like the Crazy Jane poems, to have reached to the source of things, where all speech is prophecy or song and men have the throats of birds. Stressed against the more naturalistic dialogue, they repeat in this relationship with it the continual theme of man's opposition or surrender to something "that exists, as I believe, beyond the world." Perhaps it was the experiments with prose in *The Resurrection, The Words upon the Window-pane, The Player Queen,* and the translations from Sophocles that finally ruined the careful manners characteristic of his earlier speakers. The versification of *Purgatory* and *The Herne's Egg* escapes entirely from blank verse, and the diction of all the last plays has range and freedom without losing the vigorous preoccupation with solidity of statement. The voices, unlike those in *The Shadowy Waters* or *The King's Threshold,* are not dreaming but defining and their every accent tells this.

The constant theme of Yeats's plays is the encounter between human life and some other reality to which it is linked by desire, or terror, or the longing to be complete. He brings his forces from opposite sides across that tiny, precious area the stage, and there creates the dance: the rigid, interlocking pattern, or the fight which one loses and the other wins, or the moment of revelation, "miracle." *Calvary* represents the first kind of structure, *The Herne's Egg* the second, *The Resurrection* the third. Nearly all his plays belong to the second or third kinds, and plainly not too much is to be made of the structural likenesses and differences between them, except when it is necessary to claim for these plays the possession of a *dramatic rhythm*—a movement towards, an encounter, followed by an untying, a disengagement, or even a metamorphosis. Yeats's wish "to show events and not merely tell of them"[41] was implemented in practical fashion by his long and varying studies of everything that contributes to the creation of visual experience: the movements of the body, the setting of the scene. But above all he

H

understood that the stage is a space staked out beneath the actor's feet, to be held and to be crossed, and that the business of the dramatist is not to meditate or to soliloquise, but to arrange meetings.

REFERENCES

1. *E.*, p. 250.
2. *F.P.D.*, p. 105.
3. *E.*, p. 254.
4. *E.*, pp. 249, 257.
5. T. S. Eliot, *Selected Essays*, (1934 edn.) pp. 14–15.
6. *E. & I.*, pp. 227, 231–2.
7. *E. & I.*, p. 243.
8. *E. & I.*, pp. 231, 226.
9. *C.P.*, p. 375.
10. *F.P.D.*, p. 87.
11. *E. & I.*, p. 226.
12. *F.P.D.*, p. 87.
13. See *E.*, p. 155.
14. Described by F. Kermode, Chapter IV of his *Romantic Image* (1957), and see also Gordon and Fletcher ed., *Images of a Poet* (1961), pp. 120–23.
15. *E. & I.*, pp. 224–5.
16. *E. & I.*, p. 273.
17. *Yeats's Iconography* (1960), p. 218.
18. *E. & I.*, p. 236.
19. *C.P.*, p. 266.
20. *C. Plays*, p. 217.
21. *C. Plays*, p. 215.
22. *C. Plays*, p. 218.
23. *F.P.D.*, p. vi.
24. *V.*, (1937), p. 135.
25. *C. Plays*, p. 291.
26. See above, p. 76.
27. *V.* (1937), p. 129.
28. *C. Plays*, p. 295.
29. *V.* (1937), p. 268.
30. *C. Plays*, p. 594.
31. See E. Miner, *The Japanese Tradition in British and American Literature* (Princeton, 1958), p. 260.
32. See above, p. 82.
33. See the interpretations of T. R. Henn, *The Lonely Tower* (1950), p. 270, F. Kermode, *Romantic Image*, pp. 80–81, F. A. C. Wilson, *W. B. Yeats and Tradition* (1958), pp. 71 ff.
34. Quoted by Ellmann, *The Identity of Yeats* (1954), p. 43, from an uncollected article in *Bookman*, August, 1894.
35. *C. Plays*, pp. 675–76.
36. See above, p. 37.
37. *C. Plays*, p. 698.
38. *C. Plays*, p. 689.
39. *M.*, p. 328.
40. *E. & I.*, p. 222.
41. *F.P.D.*, p. 86.

CHAPTER VII

LAST POEMS

The last plays, from *The King of the Great Clock Tower* to *Purgatory*, sometimes appear in their relatively careful organisation to contrast strangely with the general impression made by the poems of these same final years. For the poems are often reckless and excited; their style flouts many conventions of diction and metre, and tumbles about, exalted and gawky and violent; they often thrust out into a march or into a crackle of jokes; the "sixty year-old smiling public man," with his comfortable irony, has become a "wild old wicked man," the whiffler who stalks about in front of the circus-parade, "Malachi Stilt-Jack":

These new men are goldsmiths working with a glass screwed into one eye, whereas we stride ahead of the crowd, its swordsmen, its jugglers, looking to right & left.[1]

The Steinach operation in 1934 was followed by bursts of energy, sexual, political, and poetic, and he challenged his various illnesses by his own revolt against "passive suffering," which led to the notorious comment on Wilfred Owen in the Introduction to the *Oxford Book of Modern Verse* ("passive suffering is not a theme for poetry"[2]). Yeats had no desire to be taken for a quiet-voiced elder and his last period had little of the gracious serenity or autumnal calm which is attributed to poets who have reached the heights. "Indignation," he told Dorothy Wellesley, "is a kind of joy. . . . We that are joyous need not be afraid to denounce."[3] He took a great deal of pleasure in denouncing, raging, and, if Monk Gibbon's account of the way the *Oxford Book* was compiled is fair,[4] in unkindly exercising the power over other poets which his fame made possible. He thought much about politics and the state of civilisation and wrote *On the Boiler* (1938) not in a mood of reminiscence but in order to give Ireland his advice about such matters as public education and the army. He writes from Dublin to Mrs Shakespear in 1933:

> At the moment I am trying, in association with [an] ex-cabinet minister, an eminent lawyer, and a philosopher, to work out a social theory which can be used against Communism . . . what looks likes emerging is Fascism modified by religion. This country is exciting.[5]

The stress on sexuality, the taste for politics, the interest in civilisation, the discovery of the new poets of the nineteen-thirties—all these various fragmentary energies, which belong to an inflowing tide, seem at first to contrast with the feeling that this period is none the less a final period in no merely chronological sense: that Yeats's poetic mind was on the last things, and that he was perfecting a design and resolving his experience into a last, recognisable gesture. This paradox may be examined as it reveals itself in the poems.

"I am old, I belong to mythology," declares the Old Man in the Prologue of *The Death of Cuchulain*. He is one of the many *personae* by whom Yeats projects the theme of old age, which it is not surprising to find as a dominant one in the last phase. But by means of their very multiplicity he kept the theme fluid and dramatic. "Bodily decrepitude is wisdom," but it is also the return of Oisin, who refuses in *his* old age to be false to his heroic allegiances. Yeats invented Ribh, the speaker of "Supernatural Songs," another dueller with St Patrick. Ribh's mind is much on the last things; he contemplates heaven but he also invades it with his definitions. In "Ribh at the Tomb of Baile and Aillinn" he is looking at a "miraculeuse nuit nuptiale," the lovers who blaze in heavenly joy beyond the world, and receives this calmly, turning the leaves of his holy book (the works of Berkeley or Swedenborg rather than the Bible) in the light that they shed; he accepts the separation of supernatural from natural— only to deny it in the next poem. Ribh lives at the stroke of midnight when the soul is brought to God stripped of everything, swept clear of all abstractions by the passion of hatred which burns up definitions, for "where there is nothing there is God":

> Thought is a garment and the soul's a bride
> That cannot in that trash and tinsel hide.[6]

But God himself is meanwhile being redefined with terminology out of Plotinus and Madame Blavatsky ("Ribh Denounces Patrick"). Ribh uses his sight, purified by ascetic discipline, and his wisdom, magnified by old age, to see God in history as well as in heaven—to see God as a dramatist arranging a play of whose meaning the characters are ignorant ("Whence Had They Come?"), and who, as the destroyer and re-maker of civilisations is not easily distinguishable from "man's thought" itself ("Meru"). By means of Ribh, Yeats insists on keeping his eschatology down in the arena, at the meeting-place of Zeus and Leda. It is fundamental to the nature of his thought that the "Supernatural Songs" should end with poems about history and civilisation.

Yeats, in his quest for universalism and correspondences, had always wished for communication with "that which lies beyond the world" and had mirrored it in his imagination in hundreds of guises: the traditional Christian heaven, the "divine homestead" and "gates of pearl" of *The Countess Kathleen* and the early poems, the otherworldly Ocean of *The Shadowy Waters*, the Tir-nan-Og of *The Wanderings of Oisin* and Aleel, Red Hanrahan's heaven whose music is a continual clashing of swords, the purgatory and "dreaming-back" of the Noh plays, where life after death is a corridor that leads back to life on earth, the holy city of Byzantium which it is hard to distinguish from the kingdom of the perfected human imagination, the ἐκεῖ of "Supernatural Songs" where "Godhead on Godhead in sexual spasm begot/Godhead."[7] All these places, as they draw nearer and nearer to the patterns of human life, become more and more dynamic, fields of force pressing at the barriers of that life. Throughout, these forces constantly manifest themselves in acts of intervention when the supernatural descends into human life: at first their forms are traditional—the Irish and folk-tale demonology of *The Countess Kathleen*, the vaguer archangels and Danaan hosts of the early poems, the Angel of *The Hour-Glass*, who are only messengers of heaven or hell. But as Yeats begins to classify men as images of his convictions, the ages in which they live become more important and more distinguishable from one another by historical description; men are put into history. History itself, at whatever cost to the individual, becomes more and more the object of these divine visitations which take more precise and less orthodox forms: the unicorn, the beast-god, the Pantocrator who destroys Greece and Rome. In the end, the whole process becomes one: the gyres of history interlock with miracle, the individual life passes continually back and forth from nature to supernature. The divine has no other function but to arrange the drama—or the dance—of human life; it is the fabulous artificer of men and civilisations or even simply a kind of metaphor for some constant drive or impulse which orders their changing styles and temperaments:

> Measurement began our might:
> Forms a stark Egyptian thought,
> Forms that gentler Phidias wrought.

> Michael Angelo left a proof
> On the Sistine chapel roof,
> Where but half-awakened Adam
> Can disturb globe-trotting Madam
> Till her bowels are in heat,
> Proof that there's a purpose set
> Before the secret working mind:
> Profane perfection of mankind.[8]

At times Yeats seems ready to say that man creates everything not only the character of his individual incarnations out of his own soul but that of his successive
civilisations out of the racial memory, the *anima mundi*:
"we must hold to what we have that the next civilisation
may be born, not from a virgin's womb, nor a tomb without a body, not from a void, but of our own rich experience":[9]

> Death and life were not
> Till man made up the whole,
> Made lock, stock and barrel
> Out of his bitter soul,[10]

It is natural, therefore, that both Yeats and his stylised
poetic sage at the furthest margins of life, the decorum
of whose character is to meditate upon the last things,
should think much about the state of civilisation, God's
drama, the nearest we get to any *opus dei*. "You and I
are in history, the history of the mind," he told Dorothy
Wellesley.[11] The study of this "sacred drama" serves for
what, in a more orthodox mind faced with its dissolution,
might be the preparation by means of prayer and repentance for a heaven quite different from human life.

Because this drama, as it had in "Nineteen Hundred
and Nineteen," entails the destruction of so much that
has been loved and beautiful, and because we dread
death or transformation, it is a tragedy. But here again a
deep-rooted complex of ideas comes into play, which is
summed up in Lady Gregory's phrase "Tragedy must be

a joy to the man who dies."[12] Yeats shifted about with the terms "joy," "ecstasy," and "gaiety," but had for long insisted on the links between them and the tragic character: "no actress has ever sobbed when she played Cleopatra;" the tragic character, in completing his life and consummating his image, experiences "creative joy" the antithesis of "passive suffering"—"an energy so noble, so powerful, that we laugh aloud and mock, in the terror or the sweetness of our exaltation, at death and oblivion";[13] when all falls in ruin, poetry cries out in joy, Seanchan had said, and Shakespeare's heroes display this "last playing and mockery of the victorious sword":

> only when we are gay over a thing, and can play with it, do we show ourselves its master, and have minds clear enough for strength. . . . That we may be free from all the rest, sullen anger, solemn virtue, calculating anxiety, gloomy suspicion, prevaricating hope, we should be reborn in gaiety.[14]

When, therefore, Yeats describes the ruin and rise of civilisations in the two major poems which open *Last Poems*, "The Gyres" and "Lapis Lazuli," this joy and gaiety run through the whole process, as the willed condition both of those who watch the tragic scene of history and those who play their part in it, dying or rebuilding. Not repentance or prayer, but "joyful acceptance," a gay sense of victory which transfigures the natural dread, is the spirit fitting to the sages as they contemplate the sacred drama which is the ultimate form in which man's relation to the universe presents itself to the Yeatsian imagination. He wrote to Dorothy Wellesley: "A Dutch mystic has said 'I must rejoyce, I must rejoyce without ceasing, though the whole world shudder at my joy.' Joy is the salvation of the soul." He had told her in an earlier letter:

> As you go on writing and thinking your ideas will arrange themselves. They will arrange themselves as

sand strewn upon stretched parchment does—as I have read somewhere—in reponse to a musical note. To me the supreme aim is an act of faith and reason to make one rejoice in the midst of tragedy. An impossible aim; yet I think it true that nothing can injure us.[15]

This supreme aim is his own musical note, in obedience to which many of the final poems arrange themselves. It entailed staying in history, in the "richness of experience," which is the source of new civilisation, and writing about it and for it, a joyful acceptance and a gay activity, since

> All things fall and are built again,
> And those that build them again are gay.[16]

So there is the considerable group of poems which may be called "Broadsides," although only eight of them were published as such. This was a return to the ballad and folk-song material which he had scarcely used since "The Ballad of Father Gilligan," "The Ballad of the Fox-hunter" and other poems of about 1890. These new broadsides, with their highly sophisticated use of the refrain, were intended to be sung unaccompanied before small groups of people, "as the country people sing Gaelic words, mainly for the sake of the words".[17] They include "Three Songs to the Same Tune," written for an Irish Fascist organisation, a new version of them written after his disillusionment with it ("Three Marching Songs"), "Three Songs to the One Burden," "The Curse of Cromwell," the two ballads on Roger Casement, and "Come Gather Round Me, Parnellites." These revived an old dream: "I have recovered a power of moving the common man I had in my youth. The poems I can write now will go into the general memory";[18] he remembered that the Irish Army unknowingly marched to a tune written thirty years before for "Down By the Salley Gardens." They are "poems of civilisation"

in a different sense: "A nation should be like an audience
in some great theatre . . . watching the sacred drama of
its own history," which is "the greatest of parables."[19]
They display the gaiety, freedom of diction, the sophisticated use of simple rhythms, and exemplify the joyous
energy which Yeats established as a characteristic of the
chief symbolic attitude of his old age. The sexual element
inherent in this energy and the related stylistic habits
which are an emblem of rejuvenation are found in "The
Three Bushes" and its six dependent songs, and in
"Colonel Martin," "John Kinsella's Lament for Mary
Moore," "The Wild Old Wicked Man."

> For Yeats folksong was more than a quarry for tech-
> nique or an avenue to simplicity. It represented also
> the primeval emotions of universal experience.[20]

The impulse that made the tales of *The Celtic Twilight* a
road "under the wall of Paradise to the roots of the Trees"
is at work here beneath the wit, rage and sexual bravado.
    You begin with your own village, and the cobwebs on
its walls, and reach towards universalism, Yeats had
long ago declared.[21] Rooted as usual in Ireland, his study
of the sacred drama becomes meditative and retrospective, concerned mostly with its previous acts rather than,
as with "The Gyres," its modern counter-turn, in four
major poems of the period. These, though they are influenced in varying degrees by the new bravado and
rumbustiousness, are much in the magniloquent manner
—"Parnell's Funeral," "The Municipal Gallery Revisited," "Long-Legged Fly," "The Statues." The first
of these was published in *The King of the Great Clock
Tower* with a long prose-commentary about the course of
Irish history. Katharine Tynan had told Yeats about the
falling star (she calls it a meteor) seen when Parnell was
buried,[22] and the incident suggested over forty years
later its interweaving in this poem with the myth about
the slain boy Dionysus whose heart was preserved by the

"staring virgin" (Minerva/Athene) of the song in *The
Resurrection*, Yeats's own vision of a woman shooting an
arrow at a star, and many cognate visions and stories.[23]
This rich complex of memories is organised around the
meaning "an accepted sacrifice"; Parnell is an embodiment of the sacrificial victim, boy and star, his heart
torn out, falling from the tree of life, to be reborn in
one cradle or many. The construction of this sacred
ritual-drama interlocked in myth and history, which is
the subject of the first two stanzas, is as deep as Yeats ever
goes into his own past and his elaborate reading in order
to interpret a historical incident in the light of that
"sterner eye" that looks through the historical eye,[24] the
"purpose," the force or impulse that is felt behind history
and glimpsed in Old Rocky Face in "The Gyres" or the
"dramatist" of "Whence Had They Come?" And this
force is Yeats's God, the nearest he gets to deity, something manifest in history and mythology and recognised
in their workings. In the remainder of the poem he continues the sacrificial metaphor, and makes the dramatic
metaphor explicit:

> ... popular rage,
> *Hysterica passio* dragged this quarry down.
> None shared our guilt; nor did we play a part
> Upon a painted stage when we devoured his heart.[25]

Yeats seems to have felt that it was the business of the
populace to keep their seats in the great theatre, while
they watched the sacred drama of their own history—he
quoted Victor Hugo "In the theatre the mob becomes a
people":[26] here they have invaded the stage, like any
rioting Abbey audience, or turned it into a hunting-
field, made a bloody drama of their own.

"Parnell's Funeral" is a difficult poem compared with
"A Long-Legged Fly" in which we watch the makers of
history's great images creating their reality in silent con-

centration (the queer refrain turns out, as we read, to be one of Yeats's most brilliant successes in this kind), or with "The Municipal Gallery Revisited," a majestic evocation of the *personae* of that part of Irish history which Yeats had lived through. These men and women have now become artefacts in every sense, their history transformed into a "terrible and gay" legend; in "A Bronze Head" Maud Gonne herself becomes a similar Image. But it is perhaps in "The Statues" that Yeats achieved the climactic "poem of civilisation," a great monument of unageing intellect. Here Yeats, by stating it in terms of the development of sculpture, unites his absorption in the gyres of history with his constant dwelling on the artefact as an image that embodies truth. The poem describes how the mathematics of Pythagoras ("Measurement began our might")[27] begot the statues of Phidias, and how these embodiments of ideal beauty freed from mere individual characterisation to become pure being, the austere mindless face, were chosen as objects to be loved and worshipped, as unifying images. This measured beauty ruled and shaped the history of the time; it was the impulse embodied by it which defeated Eastern formlessness at Salamis, and which, diffused in India by Alexander's conquests, helped to form the image of Buddha with its "empty" eyeballs—empty because the eyes are turned inwards in concentration on the reality of the inward life, not outwards on the confusions of appearance, "the mirror-scalèd serpent [of] multiplicity" of one of the Ribh poems.[28] Did Pearse—the poem asks and exhorts at the end—summon such an image of measured beauty in calling upon Cuchulain, the hero as unifying image, at a crisis of history in Easter 1916?

Nations, races, and individual men are unified by an image, or bundle of related images, symbolical or evocative of the state of mind, which is of all states of mind not impossible, the most difficult to that man, race, or nation.[29]

Such an archetype works in history, and the Irish— Yeats's proud, separate nation—have a special authority, amidst the raging foam and blood-dimmed tide of a dying age, to achieve "profane perfection" by uniting themselves to it. The details of the poem are hard to exhaust,[30] but they combine with extraordinary fervour and agility, and in a vividly dramatic shorthand, almost all Yeats's most urgent convictions. In it, as in "Parnell's Funeral," "The Gyres," "Whence Had They Come?" or "Meru", we glimpse yet another embodiment of the "God" or force or "dramatist" of history—all terms that are betraying because they suggest a hypostasis or an abstraction, whereas what Yeats insists upon is that history, like his dancer, has not got a soul of meaning separable from a body of accomplishment. God *is* the sacred drama, which is therefore a proper subject for last poems.

Yeats, of course, did not always so transfigure dread; he admitted that this was hardly possible, and "The Man and the Echo," for example—a predominantly fearful and melancholy poem—shows that he was right. But the poems that I have discussed seem to be those which most plainly underwrite any intention which he had of exhibiting himself in a final symbolic attitude. Redefining history, cosmic and national, as a sacred drama, which is the last insight of the Old Man, the sage, he also casts himself for the role of one of its heroes, joyous and deriding; in this way he interlaces the soul that pierces to the truth and the self that holds to the sword, "the foolish, passionate man" raging in the dark and the old man's eagle mind. This is not an attitude which can be easily refuted, because it is a virtual transformation of a life-impulse into a symbolic poem, "a self-sown, self-begotten shape":

even when the poet seems most himself . . . he is never the bundle of accident and incoherence that sits down to breakfast; he has been reborn as an idea, something intended, complete.[31]

REFERENCES

1. *L.P.*, p. 64.
2. *Oxford Book of Modern Verse* (1936), p. xxxiv; cp. *L.P.*, p. 124.
3. *L.P.*, p. 126.
4. M. Gibbon, *The Masterpiece and the Man* (London, 1959), pp. 179–84.
5. *L.*, pp. 808–9.
6. *C.P.*, p. 330.
7. *C.P.*, p. 329.
8. *C.P.*, p. 399.
9. *E.*, p. 437.
10. *C.P.*, p. 223.
11. *L.P.*, p. 149.
12. *E. & I.*, p. 523.
13. *E. & I.*, p. 322.
14. *E. & I.*, pp. 254, 252.
15. *L.P.*, pp. 126, 13.
16. *C.P.*, p. 339.
17. *On the Boiler*, (Dublin, n.d. [1938]), p. 36.
18. *L.P.*, p. 135.
19. *The King of the Great Clock Tower* (Dublin, 1934), pp. 36, 37.
20. A. B. Friedman, *The Ballad Revival* (Chicago, 1962), p. 330.
21. See above, p. 30.
22. Katherine Tynan, *Twenty-Five Years*, p. 350.
23. *A.*, pp. 372–3, 576–79; and see Henn, *The Lonely Tower*, pp. 155–56, F. A. C. Wilson, *W. B. Yeats and Tradition*, pp. 60–63.
24. *C.P.*, p. 383.
25. *C.P.*, p. 319.
26. *The King of the Great Clock Tower*, p. 36.
27. *C.P.*, p. 399.
28. *C.P.*, p. 329.
29. *A.*, pp. 194–5.
30. The best account is by F. A. C. Wilson, *Yeats's Iconography*, pp. 290–303.
31. *C.P.*, p. 245; *E. & I.*, p. 509.

CHAPTER VIII

YEATS AND THE CRITICS

But, though it is hard to refute, this symbolic attitude can, of course, be criticised or rejected. Rejection, however, has not preoccupied writers about Yeats. Between them they have managed to produce more than forty books and a countless number of articles about their author, besides many books about modern poetry or poetic drama in which he is a main topic. It is possible, if foolhardy, to claim that this criticism has a rough kind of shape. What still have claims to be the two best and simplest introductions to Yeats's poetry, Louis MacNeice's *The Poetry of W. B. Yeats* (1941) and Donald Stauffer's *The Golden Nightingale* (1949) point respectively at his Irish and his symbolist fountainheads. These two concerns have played box and cox as the self and anti-self, the objective and subjective, of a great deal of Yeats criticism. As introductions to Yeats both MacNeice and Stauffer have perhaps now been superseded by D. J. Gordon's *W. B. Yeats: Images of a Poet* (with contributions by Ian Fletcher and Frank Kermode). This was originally the catalogue of the Yeats Exhibition held at Reading and at Manchester Universities. It is full of pictures, and therefore exciting, and it has a learned commentary directed to the pictures. It shows that there is a great deal more to be found out about Yeats and his circle. More and more knowledge of this kind is especially worth having.

The shape of Yeats criticism is, however, our concern here, and its approach to his nationality on the one hand

and his symbolism on the other. The first man to write a book on Yeats was an American called Horatio Sheafe Krans (1904); he chose the significant title *William Butler Yeats and the Irish Literary Revival*. A number of writers saw Yeats in this context, and it is a thoroughly relevant one. (J. M. Hone's *William Butler Yeats: The Poet in Contemporary Ireland*, E. A. Boyd's *Ireland's Literary Renaissance*, Una Ellis-Fermor's *The Irish Dramatic Movement*, A. E. Malone's *The Irish Theatre* are some examples). But what being Irish gave to Yeats's language and sensibility is most agreeably and acutely described in the first chapter, "The Background," of T. R. Henn's *The Lonely Tower*.

It cannot be said that the insights of Henn's first chapter have been much enforced by other writers on Yeats. Katharine Tynan's *Twenty-Five Years*, Maud Gonne's *A Servant of the Queen*, D. H. Greene's and E. M. Stephens' *J. M. Synge*, Lady Gregory's *Journals*, her *Coole*, her *Our Irish Theatre*, her *Visions and Beliefs*, and her *Kiltartan History Book*, and, above all, George Moore's volumes of autobiography, with J. M. Hone's *Life of Moore*, offer the means for tracing the ironies and cross-currents of the literary movement. But no critic has yet referred to their matrix, in Irish English, linguistic and rhythmical elements in Yeats's poetic speech.

There are two biographies of Yeats, which may serve as a bridge between the two themes of symbolism and Ireland as it is found in the criticism. J. M. Hone's *W. B. Yeats 1865-1939* (1942) is the official biography, and presents Yeats very fully as a man of letters, particularly as an Irish man of letters, for Hone, an Anglo-Irishman, knew the background very well and was familiar with Yeats and his circle. It is on the whole a cheerful book, does not probe very deep, and design and contours tend to be smoothed away by Hone's steady application to his job of recording all the facts—a change of residence, a speech in the Senate, an anecdote, a tragic poem, are all woven out of the same wholesome cloth. A. N. Jeffares's *W. B. Yeats: Man and Poet* (1949, revised 1962) combines criticism with biography and follows the shape of the creative life much more exigently. It is especially valuable for its many excerpts from Yeats's unpublished papers and for the information which it provides about his reading and sources. Both Hone and Jeffares used letters to and from Yeats which were then mostly unpublished. These have since been collected together in *The Letters of W. B. Yeats* by Allan Wade (1954). It is still far from being more than a selection from the correspondence. It does not contain a single letter to Maud Gonne (these appear to be lost), but there is a recent, if somewhat conjectural, account of their relationship by Curtis Bradford, "Yeats and Maud Gonne," in *Texas Studies in Literature and Language* (1962). The correspondence with T. Sturge Moore has been edited by Ursula Bridge (1953), and reveals Yeats's confirmed habit of making a philosophical argument mean what he wants it to mean in rather Humpty Dumptyish fashion. Hone's *J. B. Yeats: Letters to his Son W. B. Yeats and Others* (1944) ought to be mentioned here; there are two other collections of J. B. Yeats's letters, and also the autobiographical fragment *Early Memories* (1922) which his son encouraged him to write. Allan Wade's edition of the letters also contains a compendious biographical account, which is much the best brief, encyclopaedic biography.

Yeats's symbolism—and the term must here include both his place in the international symbolist movement and his use of personal and inherited symbols in his work —has been much more curiously studied than his Irish affinities. Edmund Wilson's influential essay in *Axel's Castle* (1936) and the pages on Yeats in F. R. Leavis's *New Bearings in English Poetry* (1932) both emphasised Yeats's growth in maturity and power away from the aestheticism, Pre-Raphaelitism, and vagueness of the

I

eighteen-nineties, and stressed his refusal to deny intelligence and struggle. His stories of "the life of ecstatic revery," writes Wilson, "unlike the typical writings of the *fin de siècle* aesthetes, are edged with the consciousness of dangers and temptations inescapably involved in such a life."[1] There are good pages in Wilson on the development of Yeats's prose style, a subject not much discussed elsewhere. In the tradition of Wilson and Leavis, and treating also, and possibly rather over-emphasising, the direct influence of the French symbolist poets, are the chapter on Yeats in C. M. Bowra's *The Heritage of Symbolism* (1943), V. K. Narayana Menon's *The Development of W. B. Yeats* (1942), some rather sketchy pages in Enid Starkie's *From Gautier to Eliot* (1960) and a somewhat mechanical treatment by means of parallels in E. Davis's *Yeats's Early Contacts with French Poetry* (Pretoria, 1961). Much the best discussion of Yeats's vital participation in the symbolist tradition will be found in Frank Kermode's *Romantic Image* (1957). Kermode shows, amongst other matters, that the symbolist idea of what a poem should be is emblematised in recurring images in his work, especially in the images of the Dancer, the passionate and rhythmical Salome figure, whose whole body thinks, the emblem in which there is no division between meaning and form, and which has, in Arthur Symon's words "the intellectual as well as the sensuous appeal of a living symbol."

These and other matters are discussed in Richard Ellmann's two books, *Yeats: the Man and the Masks* (1948) and *The Identity of Yeats* (1954). The first of these is certainly the most ambitious book yet to have been written on Yeats. It is an attempt to weave his biography, his art, and his thought, his preoccupation with symbolism, with magic, with nationality, his resistances and his acceptances of the influences of his father, friends, and lovers, into a total description of the poet as a hero who "fought past weakness and conventionality only with the

utmost labour. His life was a continual combat, and he
chose the hardest battles when he might have chosen
easier ones."[2] The stress here is on the psychology of the
artist; what the poet made, his artefacts, tend to get
overwhelmed in that raging sea; they become largely
evidence for the case history of their maker in continuing
crisis. In his second book, Ellmann emphasises the continuity of Yeats's themes, and acutely describes the alteration in Yeats's diction and syntax that may mask this
continuity. This again is a historian's book, but it is of the
utmost value to any true estimate of his poetry and super-
sedes the work of earlier critics whose just admiration for
the later poetry of Yeats led them to neglect the roots
which so astonishingly flowered:

> he changed many elements of his verse, yet his identity
> is stamped upon them everywhere. His symbols keep
> altering, but the later symbols, in spite of their in-
> creased animation when compared to the earlier, are
> mature equivalents. . . . His heroes always remain re-
> cognizable through many transformations;[3]

Ellmann's two books bring the description of Yeats's
mind and art to a level of sophistication which has probably fixed the image of Yeats for his immediate posterity. Other books contribute more detail, often of a
very fascinating kind, to our knowledge of the literary
and pictorial sources and origins. There is no complete study of his use of Irish mythology, although the
subject comes into many books, including A. D. M.
Hoare's *The Works of Morris and of Yeats in relation to
Early Saga Literature* (1937) and Birgit Bjersby's *The
Cuchulain Legend in the Works of W. B. Yeats* (1950).
Yeats's habit of revising his poetry can now be studied in
full in *The Variorum Edition* (1957) by Peter Allt and
R. K. Alspach, a book which was to some extent antici-
pated by the study of this subject in relation to the early
poems and plays in Thomas Parkinson's *W. B. Yeats:*

Self-Critic (1951) and by Marion Witt's "Yeats's Revision of his later Poems" (*P.M.L.A.*, 1949). Ellmann in his *Identity of Yeats* and others had also written about early manuscript drafts; a recent contribution on this subject is Curtis Bradford's full and fascinating account of the manuscript drafts of the Byzantium poems (*P.M.L.A.*, 1960). The influence of painting on Yeats's poetry and the formation of his symbols was studied for the first time in T. R. Henn's *The Lonely Tower* (1950), and this gives this warmly sympathetic but rather ill-organised full-scale study of Yeats its chief importance; Giorgio Melchiori's *Whole Mystery of Art* (1960) is also acutely aware of the importance of visual material and, following Ellmann, of the continuity of Yeats's symbols. Melchiori's treatment of the formative elements that contributed to "Leda and the Swan" and "The Second Coming" organises them into a powerful demonstration of the continuity and transformation of Yeats's symbols in a way that proves, on its smaller scale, Ellmann's larger argument. Virginia Moore's *The Unicorn: William Butler Yeats's Search for Reality* (1954) has informative chapters on Yeats's Hermetic studies, on Rosicrucianism, and Yeats's readings in philosophy after he had written the first version of *A Vision*, but is unfortunately marred by an intolerable vulgarity of tone. Much more agreeably written are F. A. C. Wilson's two books *W. B. Yeats and Tradition* (1958) and *Yeats's Iconography* (1960). These are of particular interest to students of the "unresolved residues of meaning" in the plays. They uncover the sources, especially in the neo-platonic and occult traditions, of many recurrent symbols. Yeats said that his plays started off as a "bundle of ideas," but that "gradually philosophy is eliminated"; Wilson, however, desires to explain everything in terms of the subjective neo-platonic tradition, and he makes Yeats look as though he was always writing to a perfectly conscious, doctrinal programme. Wilson has immensely increased our knowledge of

Yeats's esoteric learning, but he has failed—and one can be glad that this is so—to revive the old worries about the relationship between Yeats's greatness as a poet and the eccentricity or wrongheadedness—or rightness—of his beliefs. This question is largely disposed of by Ellmann's arguments. It was a problem that bothered I. A. Richards, T. S. Eliot (in *After Strange Gods*) and Stephen Spender (in *The Destructive Element*), and lies behind W. H. Auden's question: "the reaction of most of us to all that occult is, I fancy, the same: How on earth, we wonder, could a man of Yeats's gifts take such nonsense seriously?"[4] Auden's essay is included in the volume of selected criticism edited by James Hall and Martin Steinmann *The Permanence of Yeats* (1950); the worrying theme runs through a number of the essays in this volume, but it also reprints some of the best short pieces on Yeats done before the Yeats industry entered its post-Ellmann phase, including Eric Bentley's defence of the plays. If the old worry is to be revived, it will come—has indeed already come—in the form of a questioning of the symbolist tradition itself and of the limitation, consequent upon that tradition, of the poet's right to discourse, of the way in which much modern poetry, in Graham Hough's words, "has shorn itself of paraphrasable content, of all narrative or discursive line, and relies on the play of contrasted images alone."[5] Hough exempts Yeats from this charge: "It is something of a paradox that Yeats, whose beliefs are often supposed to be more fantastic and irrational than those of any other great mind of our time, should never have lost his faith in rational order and the disposing intelligence as the guiding principle of a poem." But it is hard to see precisely where the anti-symbolist counter-revolution will lead, and it does not seem entirely unlikely that it will chip away a good deal at Yeats.

The mass of writing which Yeats's immediate posterity has produced, of which this is only a highly selective account, presents a problem for the ordinary reader of poetry. He badly needs a complete "Variorum" edition in the other sense—*cum notis variorum*, with which to solve puzzles as he reads. There are two books which go some way in this direction—G. B. Saul's *Prolegomena to the Study of Yeats's Poems* (1957) lists the poems and gives references to major critical *loci* for each poem; John Unterecker's *A Reader's Guide to W. B. Yeats*, a poem-by-poem analysis, (1959), pays very full and proper attention to the early poems as well as the later, but by underlining too rigidly Yeats's intention of arranging his poems in family units often distorts those which won't satisfactorily fit. It would have been a better book if it had consisted quite frankly of notes on each poem. This is what A. N. Jeffares has supplied for many of the major poems in his selection, *Poems of W. B. Yeats*, in the Scholar's Library series (1962). Editorial commentary of this kind is a necessary undertaking now that Yeats has, in W. H. Auden's words, 'become his admirers', for

> Now he is scattered among a hundred cities
> And wholly given over to unfamiliar affections.

REFERENCES

1. Wilson, *Axel's Castle* (New York, 1936), p. 33.
2. Ellmann, *Yeats: the Man and the Masks* (London, 1949), p. 6.
3. Ellmann, *The Identity of Yeats* (London, 1954), p. 246.
4. Hall and Steinmann, *The Permanence of Yeats* (New York, 1950), p. 345.
5. Hough, *Image and Experience* (London, 1960), p. 27.

SELECTED BIBLIOGRAPHY

I. YEATS

A complete record will be found in *A Bibliography of the Writings of W. B. Yeats*, ed. Allan Wade, London (Hart-Davis) 1958.

The major editions of the poems and plays are: *Collected Poems*, London (Macmillan) 1950; *Collected Plays*, London (Macmillan) 1952; *The Variorum Edition of the Poems*, New York (Macmillan) 1957.

The great bulk of the prose-work is reprinted in five volumes, all published by Macmillan: *Autobiographies*, 1955; *Mythologies*, 1958; *Essays and Introductions*, 1961; *A Vision*, 1961 (a reprint of the 1937 edition); *Explorations*, 1962. The major edition of the *Letters* was edited by Allan Wade, London (Hart-Davis) 1954.

These volumes do not comprise a complete collected edition of Yeats's writings. The following are amongst the most important of the volumes containing material which has not been recently reprinted: *Fairy and Folk-Tales of the Irish Peasantry*, London (Walter Scott) 1888; *Stories from Carleton*, London (Walter Scott) 1889; *Representative Irish Tales* 2 vols., New York (Knickerbocker Press) 1891; *Where There Is Nothing*, Stratford-upon-Avon (A. H. Bullen) 1903; *The Collected Works of William Butler Yeats in Verse and Prose*, 8 vols., Stratford-upon-Avon (A. H. Bullen) 1908; *Four Plays for Dancers*, London (Macmillan) 1921; *Plays and Controversies*, London (Macmillan) 1923; *A Vision*, London (T. W. Laurie) 1925; *Letters to the New Island* ed. Horace Reynolds, Cambridge, Mass. (Harvard University Press) 1934; *The Ten Principal Upanishads* (with Shri Purohit Swami), London (Faber & Faber) 1937; *On the Boiler*, Dublin (Cuala Press) 1938; *Letters on Poetry from W. B. Yeats to Dorothy Wellesley*, London (Oxford University Press) 1940.

II. OTHERS

Two surveys of Yeats criticism are by A. N. Jeffares in *Hermathena*, LXXII (1948), and Hazard Adams in *Texas Studies in Literature and Language*, III (1962). The fullest select bibliography (up to 1950 only) will be found in *The Permanence of Yeats* (listed below), and there is a shorter one (up to 1957) in G. B. Saul's *Prolegomena* (listed below). In the case of books published in both the United States and Britain the date of the British edition is given.

ADAMS, HAZARD: *Blake and Yeats: the Contrary Vision*, Ithaca, New York 1955.

ALSPACH, RUSSELL K.: "Some Sources of Yeats's *The Wanderings of Oisin*" in *Publications of the Modern Language Association*, LVIII (1943), 849 ff.

BAYLEY, JOHN: *The Romantic Survival*, London 1957.

BJERSBY, BIRGIT: *The Cuchulain Legend in the Works of W. B. Yeats*, Uppsala 1950.

BRADFORD, CURTIS: "Yeats's Byzantium Poems: A Study of their Development" in *Publications of the Modern Language Association*, LXXV (1960), 110 ff.

——: "Yeats and Maud Gonne," in *Texas Studies in Language and Literature*, III (1962), 452 ff.

BOWRA, C. M.: *The Heritage of Symbolism*, London 1943.

BOYD, ERNEST A.: *Ireland's Literary Renaissance*, London and Dublin 1916.

ELLIS-FERMOR, UNA: *The Irish Dramatic Movement*, London, second edition 1954.

ELLMANN, RICHARD: *Yeats the Man and the Masks*, London 1949.

——: *The Identity of Yeats*, London 1954.

FRYE, NORTHROP: "Yeats and the Language of Symbolism," in *University of Toronto Quarterly*, XVII.

GIBBON, MONK: *The Masterpiece and the Man: Yeats as I Knew Him*. London 1959.

GORDON, D. J. ed.: W. B. Yeats: *Images of a Poet*, London 1961.

HALL, JAMES AND STEINMANN, MARTIN edd.: *The Permanence of Yeats: Selected Criticism*, New York 1950.

HENN, T. R.: *The Lonely Tower: Studies in the Poetry of W. B. Yeats*, London 1950.

——: "The Accent of Yeats's *Last Poems*," in *Essays and Studies of the English Association*, IX (1956).

HOARE, DOROTHY M.: *The Works of Morris and of Yeats in Relation to Early Saga Literature*, Cambridge 1937.

HONE, JOSEPH: *William Butler Yeats: the Poet in Contemporary Ireland*, London 1916.

——: *W. B. Yeats 1865–1939*, London 1942.

HOUGH, GRAHAM: *The Last Romantics*, London 1949.

JEFFARES, A. NORMAN: *W. B. Yeats, Man and Poet*, London 1949, 1962.

——: *The Poetry of W. B. Yeats*, London 1961.

——: "The Byzantine Poems of W. B. Yeats," [with Select Bibliography] *English Studies in Africa*, V (1962), 11 ff.

KERMODE, FRANK: *Romantic Image*, London 1957.

KRANS, HORATIO SHEAFE: *William Butler Yeats and the Irish Literary Revival*, London 1905.

LEAVIS, F. R.: *New Bearings in English Poetry*, London 1932.

MACNEICE, LOUIS: *The Poetry of W. B. Yeats*, London 1941.

MARTIN, GRAHAM: "The Later Poetry of W. B. Yeats" in *The Modern Age* (Pelican Guide to English Literature), ed. B. Ford, London 1961.

MALONE, A. E.: *The Irish Theatre*, London 1939.

MELCHIORI, GIORGIO: *The Whole Mystery of Art: Pattern into Poetry in the Work of W. B. Yeats*, London 1960.

MENON, V. K. NARAYANA: *The Development of William Butler Yeats*, Edinburgh and London 1942.

MINER, EARL: *The Japanese Tradition in British and American Literature*, Princeton 1958.

MOORE, VIRGINIA: *The Unicorn: William Butler Yeats' Search for Reality*, New York 1954.

PARKINSON, THOMAS: *W. B. Yeats Self-Critic*, Berkeley and Los Angeles 1951.

——: "The World of Yeats's 'Nineteen Hundred and Nineteen'," *University of California Publications, English Studies*, XI (1955), 211 ff.

SAUL GEORGE BRANDON: *Prolegomena to the Study of Yeats's Poems*, Philadelphia 1957.

STAUFFER, DONALD A: *The Golden Nightingale*, New York 1949.

STOCK, A. G.: *W. B. Yeats his Poetry and Thought*, Cambridge 1961.

UNTERECKER, JOHN: *A Reader's Guide to William Butler Yeats*, London 1959.

URE, PETER: *Towards a Mythology: Studies in the Poetry of W. B. Yeats*, Liverpool and London 1946.

——: *Yeats the Playwright*, London 1963.

WILSON, EDMUND: "W. B. Yeats" in *Axel's Castle*, New York 1936.

WILSON, F. A. C.: *W. B. Yeats and Tradition*, London 1958.

——: *Yeats's Iconography*, London 1960.

WITT, MARION: "The Making of an Elegy: Yeats's 'In Memory of Major Robert Gregory'," in *Modern Philology*, XLVIII (1949), 112 ff.

——: "A Competition for Eternity: Yeats's Revision of his Later Poems," in *Publications of the Modern Language Association*, LXIV (1949), 40 ff.